T0131457

31 DAYS OF EFFECTUAL PRAYER

Tramara Murray

authorHOUSE®

AuthorHouse™
1663 Liberty Drive
Bloomington, IN 47403
www.authorhouse.com
Phone: 1 (800) 839-8640

Published by AuthorHouse 07/25/2018

ISBN: 978-1-5462-5191-0 (sc)
ISBN: 978-1-5462-5189-7 (hc)
ISBN: 978-1-5462-5190-3 (e)

Library of Congress Control Number: 2018908512

Print information available on the last page.

Any people depicted in stock imagery provided by Getty Images are models, and such images are being used for illustrative purposes only. Certain stock imagery © Getty Images.

This book is printed on acid-free paper.

Scripture taken from The Holy Bible, King James Version. Public Domain

31 DAYS OF EFFECTUAL PRAYER

For the dedicated Christian

All Glory and Honor to my Lord and Savior Jesus.

This book is dedicated to my mother

CONTENTS

INTRODUCTION

At age 5, I was called to learn intercessory prayer from my mother. Every day the Father would summon my mother to convene with him for communion. The communion of bread and wine in remembrance to our Lord & Savior Jesus, is not that of which I speak. I'm speaking of communion as in having a conversation with someone.

So, there I was a little girl kneeling beside my mother. As she was praying, the seed of the Word of God was being embedded in my spirit. Grateful for my experience, I have been a prophetic Intercessor for over 20 years. Glory to God! This prayer manual is dedicated to my mother who has gone home to be with our Heavenly Father. To my surprise the Father later began to call for those seeds to come forth.

As you began to pray with me from this book ask the Holy Spirit to give you a Spirit of Prayer and a Spirit of Worship. We have our own personal struggles in which we need deliverance. Pray the prayers from this book alone. Also, pray the prayers from this book with other family members, especially on the behalf of another. When a loved one is struggling with something that has a stronghold on them, a group can together bombard heaven for that loved one's deliverance.

While writing this book, I continually asked Holy Spirit to give me what I should say. I pray that the words written will be a blessing to you. This prayer manual also requires your Worship before reading each prayer. The lyrics to the songs are provided on the page before each prayer topic. If you have access to a computer or a smart phone go to www.youtube.com and type in the names of each song listed. You will experience prayer like you never have before. I recommend that you engage in prayer daily, and after repeating the prayer, sing a closing song. Then watch God move in your situation. Before you read this book pray this prayer: Father we love you, we need you, we can do nothing without you, have mercy on us, wash us, purge us and cleanse us. Father please forgive us of our sins and make us new in you. In Christ Jesus' name we pray, Amen.

It is Well with My Soul
When peace like a river, attendeth my way,
When sorrows like sea billows roll
Whatever my lot, thou hast taught me to say
It is well, it is well, with my soul
It is well
With my soul
It is well, it is well with my soul
Though Satan should buffet, though trials should come,

I Will Trust in the Lord – see lyrics on line
(Various Performers)

I Surrender All – see lyrics on line
(Various Performers)

PRAYER FOR CHURCH BODY

Let us sing our 3 Worship songs to Usher us into the Presence of God:

It is Well with My Soul
I Will Trust in the Lord
I Surrender All

Prayer: Heavenly Father, we come before your throne of grace today in humble adoration, praise and worship. We come to say we love you, we need you, and we look to you Father for our guidance, our strength, our wisdom. Father, we realize that without you we can do nothing. Father, we are asking for your divine intervention. We realize that we haven't walked according to your plan and purpose for our lives. Today Father God, we humbly ask for your forgiveness. We ask you to wash us, purge us, cleanse us from all unrighteousness and create in us a clean heart and renew the right Spirit within us. (Psalms 51) God, you said if we ask for forgiveness that you would forgive us of our sins and cleanse us from all unrighteousness. (1 John 1v9) So we now say thank you Father for forgiving us. We come today presenting our petitions before you God. We come today on behalf of the Church Universal. Father we come today asking that you make it clear to us who we are and what we should do? Help us to stay focused on this journey and help us to stay on the right path. We are praying God, for an awakening. Asking you Father to help us love as you love. Help us forgive as you forgive. Father, we pray to be one as you and the Father are one. (John 10v30) Father, we your people are in need of a revival. We need to be rebuked, reproved, to be resuscitated and restored. We need clarity of sight, clarity of thought, clarity of mind, and clarity of the times. Father help us to be reconciled back to you and your Word. (2 Cor 5v18,19) We pray that our hearts will be turned to you first. And then Father, turn our hearts back to our spouses and our families. Father, help us to love each other in your house so that the world will see our love for one another and desire to be a part of that fold. (John 13v34,35, Gal 6v10) Father, help us do all you have called us to do. Father put the right people in our lives to help us grow, to teach us how to pray, and teach us how to live. Father, we pray that you would write your Holy Words on the canvas of our hearts. Help us to not sin against you. Father, show us those things and areas that we desire to hang on to. It is those things that we have made our friends that don't please you. Father, please help us! Holy Spirit please work in the hearts and minds of us, your people. Holy Spirit draw us closer to you Oh God! Father, quicken us with a Spirit of Repentance! Help us to not just be hearers of your word but also doers Father God. (Jam 1v22) Father, you said we have not because we asked not. We are asking you for all these things today. Your word says your ears are open to the cry of the righteous (1 Pet 3 v 12). Thank you, Father, in advance for hearing us. It is in Jesus' name we pray. Amen

Notes to Self

The Old Rugged Cross
On a hill far away, stood an old rugged Cross
The emblem of suffering and shame
And I love that old Cross where the dearest and best
For a world of lost sinners was slain

So, I'll cherish the old rugged Cross
Till my trophies at last I lay down
I will cling to the old rugged Cross
And exchange it someday for a crown

Count Your Blessings – see lyrics on line
(Performed by Johnson Oatman and J.R.)

I Have Decided to Follow Jesus – see lyrics on line
(Various Performers)

PRAYER FOR THE NATIONS

Let us sing our 3 Worship songs to Usher us into the Presence of God:

The Old Rugged Cross
Count Your Blessings
I Have Decided to Follow Jesus

Prayer: Heavenly Father we come before your throne of grace today as humble as we know how. We come in a spirit of thanksgiving, praise, and honor. All the praises, glory and honor are due to you in the name of Jesus. Father, we come bowing our hearts in your presence as we say thank you. Father, we thank you for life, health, and strength. Father, we thank you for the blood running warm in my veins. We thank you for the healing of our body. We thank you for every organ functioning the way you created it to operate. Thank you, Father! This is the day the Lord hath made and we will rejoice and be glad in it. (Ps 118v24) This is a day we have never seen before. Father, we thank you for saving us and our extended family. We thank you for leading us, guiding us and protecting us. We thank you for your continuous blessings. Father, you bless us even when we don't deserve it. Father, we need you! We can't make it on our own. We need your help God! We realize that we can do nothing without you God. Father, have mercy on us! We need your wisdom, your guidance, your love and your strength. Father, please forgive us for our sins. Father, you said if we ask for forgiveness you would be faithful and just to forgive us and cleanse us from all unrighteousness. (1 John 1v9) Father, today we come before you to lift up this and other nations Oh God. Father God your word said that we should make intercession and supplications, and giving of thanks for all kings, and for all that are in authority; that we may lead a quiet and peaceable life in all godliness and honesty. For this is good and acceptable in the sight of God our Savior. (1 Tim 2v1-3) Father, we need you God! Help us we are your children! Father scripture said if we, your people who are called by your name, shall humble themselves, and pray, seek your face, and turn from their wicked ways; then we will hear from heaven, and you will forgive our sins, and you will heal our land. (2 Chron 7v14) We are crying out to you God help us! We need you God, this nation needs you God, our governments need you God. Father we are praying for righteousness to prevail in every nation, we are praying for unity across party lines. Father, scriptures say the people are destroyed for lack of knowledge. Father, we are praying for your divine intervention, instructions and guidance. Holy Spirit we pray that you move on the hearts and minds of all people. Holy Spirit we pray that you bring conviction, deliverance and your love. Draw us close to you Father. We can't do anything without God. (John 15v5B) You said we have not, because we ask not. (James 4v2) We are asking in faith. And we thank you in advance for hearing our prayers. It is in Jesus' name we pray. Amen

Notes to Self

What a Friend We Have in Jesus
What a friend we have in Jesus
All our sins and griefs to bear
And what a privilege to carry
Everything to God in prayer
Oh, what peace we often forfeit
Oh, what needless pain we bear
All because we do not carry
Everything to God in prayer

Jesus, I love Calling Your Name – see lyrics on line
(Various Performers)

As the Deer Panteth for the Water – see lyrics on line
(Written by Martin J. Nystrom)

PRAYER FOR WHAT LIES AHEAD

Let us sing our 3 Worship songs to Usher us into the Presence of God:

What a Friend We Have in Jesus
Jesus I Love Calling Your Name
As the Deer Panteth For the Water

Prayer: Heavenly Father, we come before your throne of Grace today to say thank you. Thank you for life, health and strength. Thank you for your grace and mercy. Thank you for the roof over our heads, the clothes on our backs and the shoes for our feet. Father, we thank you for clean running water. Father, we thank you for never leaving us and for never forsaking us. Father, we love you, we praise you and we bless your Holy Name. Father we need you and we know we can't make it without you, Oh God! Father, we now ask you to forgive us of our sins. Father, sometimes we lie, walk in the spirit of unforgiveness, and even steal. Father, we even ignore what you've have asked us to do, and sometimes we go right on and do those things you've ask us not to do. Help us Father! We are a mess and we need you Oh God! Father, we realize that we can't do this without you! Father, if you don't go before us we can't go. (Ex 33v15) Your wisdom and your knowledge Father, is so unfathomable, and your understandings are so unsearchable. Father, there is nothing too hard for you. (Gen 18v14) Father, you put these bodies together so perfectly. Father, you are he who put together the universe, and they still obey your command from creation. Father, when you hung the stars and moon you commanded them to be still and they still obey to this day. Father, you know everything about everything. Father, you even know what lies ahead. You can even see what is going on in the last days right now today. So, Father, today we ask you to prepare our hearts and mind for those days ahead, oh God. (Isa. 46v8-10) Father, your Word says that you have declared the former things from

9

the beginnings and that from the beginning declared it to thee; before it came to pass I shewed it thee. And that thou hast heard, seen all this; and will not yet declare it? I have shewed thee new things from this time, even hidden things, and thou didst not know them and that they are created now, and not from the beginning. (Isa 48) Father, we know that you are trying to show us and tell us these things Oh God, but we don't heed your instructions because of our stiff neck edness. (Math. 13v15) Oh God, how we need you so desperately to forgive us. Father, we need you so desperately to cleanse us, protect us, strengthen us and fight for us. Father, you told Moses if you could find fifty righteous you would spare Sodom and Gomorrah. (Gen. 18v26) Father, we are praying and asking for your protection and covering on behalf of the righteous. Father, reveal your secrets to us as only you can God. Do it Father for those that have your heart. Do it for those who live in a place of repentance and a place of self-examination Oh God. Father, help us to wake up from our sleep, and be ready for what lies ahead. Help us God! Father, we are praying for supernatural strength, endurance and perseverance. Father, help us! Father, you are getting ready to remove that one that is holding back the Lawless one. (2 Thes. 2v7) Father, you said you won't do anything until you first reveal it to your servants the Prophets. (Amos 3v7) Father, please circumcise our hearts and minds. Father, we pray that we your children will be ready. You said we have not because we ask not. But today Father we are asking, please grant us our petitions. We ask you all these things in your son Jesus' name. Amen

Notes to Self

There is Power in the Blood
Would you be free from the burden of sin?
There's power in the blood, power in the blood
Would you o'er evil a victory win?
There's wonderful power in the blood
There is power, power, wonder-working power
In the blood of the Lamb
There is power, power, wonder-working power
In the precious blood of the Lamb

Open the Eyes of my Heart – see lyrics on line
(written by Paul Baloche, performed by various artists)

Welcome into this Place – see lyrics on line
(This song is performed by various artists)

PRAYER FOR OUR COMMUNITY

Let us sing our 3 Worship songs to Usher us into the Presence of God:

There is Power in the Blood
Open the Eyes of My Heart
Welcome into This Place

Prayer: Heavenly Father, we come before your throne of grace today to say thank you. Thank you for life, health and strength. Thank you for sending your son Jesus to die for us on Calvary cross. Thank you, Father! Thank you! Today Father, we come to say we love you, we need you and we can't make it without you. Father, all the glory, honor and praises all day that belong to you, Oh God. Father, you are majestic, you are holy, and you are righteous. Father, forgive us for our sins. Sometimes Father we sin with our mouth. And we sin with our heart. Forgive us for the sins of hatred, anger, unforgiveness. Father, help us! Father, today we come lifting-up our community. Father, we ask you to help us to be your hands extended. Help us to be your voice in the Earth. We pray God to be a source of encouragement for those who don't know you. Help us God to let our light shine in this dark place. Father, let them see our good works so that they will glorify you. (1 Pet 2v12) You said Father God, when we lift-up the name of Jesus that you would draw all men to you. Holy Spirit, I ask you to draw them in. Jesus your name is the name that is above all names. (Phillip 2v9,10) Scripture says demons hear the name called Jesus and they shudder. (Jam 2v19) The scriptures say that at the name of Jesus every knee will bow and every tongue will confess that Jesus is Lord. (Rom 14v11) Holy Spirit, we ask you now to walk up and down every street, every road in every city and pull on the heartstrings of every believer/unbeliever. We ask you Holy Spirit to visit every home, every family and every community touch every heart God and break up the fallow ground therein. (Hosea

10v12) Father, restore our hearts and minds. Father, remove every hurt, remove bitterness, unforgiveness and hatred. Father, do it for your glory. Father, we pray a blood covering over every community. Protect them from gun violence, gang violence, drugs and alcohol addiction. We rebuke the spirit of poverty from the hearts and minds of those in our communities in the name of Jesus. Father, we pray for every first born male child in these homes, where there is no father figure help them to be the spiritual leaders of these homes. Father, we pray that your word would be a lamp unto their feet and light for their pathways. (Ps. 119v105) I pray for strength to every area of their lives, Oh God. Help them Father to draw strength from other mature Godly males and their families, Oh God. Help them to love each other and pray for each other, Oh God. Help them to stay locked in to your Word, Oh God! Help them Oh God, to endeavor to keep the unity in the bonds of peace. (Eph. 4v3). Father, you said your ears are open to the prayers of the righteous (1 Pet 3v12). You said we have not because we ask not, but we are asking in faith today; and we thank you in advance Father. In Jesus' name we pray. Amen

Notes to Self

How Great thou Art
Oh Lord my God
When I in awesome wonder
Consider all the worlds
Thy hands have made
I see the stars
I hear the rolling thunder
Thy power throughout
The universe displayed

All to Jesus I Surrender – see lyrics on line
(written by Judson W. Van DeVenter, performed by various artists)

Go Tell it on the Mountain – see lyrics on line
(Various Performers)

PRAYER FOR FAMILIES

Let us sing our 3 Worship songs to Usher us into the Presence of God:

How Great Thou Art
All to Jesus I Surrender
Go Tell It on the Mountain

Prayer: Heavenly Father we come before your throne of Grace today to say thank you. We thank you Father for life, health, and strength. Father, we thank you for our very breath. We thank you that our organs are working properly. We thank you for the blood running warm through our veins. We thank you that all our bills are paid, and all of our needs are met. We thank you for the roof over our heads. We thank you for the clothes on our backs and shoes for our feet. We thank you Father for clean running water. Father, we need you and our families need you Oh God! Father, we need you to lead us, guide us, comfort us, protect us and walk with us Father. Those on our job need you God. Those in our church need you God. Those in the hospital need you God. Father, those in jail or in prison cells, they need you. We pray Father that you will walk up and down every corridor of the hospital and the jail/prisons to touch, heal and deliver. Father, we ask you for forgiveness of our sins. Father, forgive us for sins of omission and our sins of commissions. You said if we ask for forgiveness you would be faithful and just to forgive us and cleanse us from all unrighteousness. (1 John 1v9) Father, we pray that the church will teach younger men to follow after the example of righteous older men. Help us Father to teach them to be temperate, worthy of respect, self-controlled, and sound in faith, in love and in endurance. Also, Father, help our older women to be teachers for the younger women. Help them to teach the younger women to be respectful in the way they live, not to be slanderous but to teach what is good. That they must lead by example. We pray that the younger women will be taught how to love their husbands and children. We pray for them to be self-controlled and pure, and to be busy at home, to be kind, and to be subject to their husbands, so that no one will malign the word of God. Teach us to walk with integrity, seriousness and soundness of speech that cannot be condemned, so that those who oppose us may be ashamed because they have nothing bad to say about us. Help us to respect those in authority over us in everything, and to try to please them, serving as unto the Lord and not to talk back to them, and not to steal from them, but to show that we can be fully trusted, so that in every way they will make the teaching about God our Savior attractive. (Titus 2v1-10) Father, your Word says that if we believe on the Lord Jesus Christ that us and our households would be saved. (Acts 16v31) Father, we pray that you would remove the scales from their eyes and that you would unstop their ears to that they may see and hear and be converted. (Isa 35v5) Father, have mercy on us your people Oh God! Father, we pray that you move by your Spirit over this land, and through our cities and in our homes. Father, help us Lord! We have strayed so far from you and from your Holy Words. Father, we pray that you pour out the former and latter rain in our lives Oh God. We should not look to the left or the right but continue to look straight ahead. (Isa 30v21) Father, you said we have not because we ask not. Father, today we ask for your divine intervention. And we ask you all these things in your son Jesus' name. Amen

Notes to Self

Tis so Sweet to Trust in Jesus
'Tis so sweet to trust in Jesus,
Just to take Him at His Word
Just to rest upon His promise,
Just to know, "Thus saith the Lord!"
Jesus, Jesus, how I trust Him!
How I've proved Him o'er and o'er
Jesus, Jesus, precious Jesus!
Oh, for grace to trust Him more!

You are my All in All – see lyrics on line
(Performed by Dennis Jernigan)

Go tell it on the Mountain – see lyrics on line
(is an African-American spiritual song)

PRAYER FOR MARRIAGES

Let us sing our 3 Worship songs to Usher us into the Presence of God:

Tis so Sweet to Trust in Jesus
You Are My All in All
Go Tell It on the Mountain

Prayer: Heavenly Father we come before your throne of grace today to say thank you. Thank you, Father. Thank you for life, health and strength. Thank you for our families. Thank you for our church family. Thank you for this new day. Thank you for the blood flowing warm in our veins. Father we thank you for another opportunity to tell someone about your saving grace. It is another opportunity to be your hands and hearts extended here on this Earth. Father forgive us for our sins. We have committed sins of omission and sins of commissions. Sometimes Father we sin with our mouth and we sin with our heart. Father, forgive us. You said if we ask for forgiveness you would forgive us. (1 John 1v9) So Father we say thank you again for another chance to do it right. Father, today we come to you lifting up every marriage all over the land. Father, cover every marriage that has been committed to your hand; we pray that they will experience a closer walk with you. We pray that they will receive a double portion of your anointing for forgiveness, kindness, tenderness, gentleness, and longsuffering. Teach them how to communicate effectively. Teach them how to nurture, respect and cherish each other. Father, teach the husband that he is supposed to love his wife as Christ loved the church. (Eph. 5v25) Also teach the wife that she must submit to her husband as unto the Lord in those things that are right and honorable before the Lord. Father, please remember those marriages that haven't been committed to your hand. We pray God that Holy Spirit would tug on the heartstrings of those that are far from you to desire a relationship with you Father God. We pray that they will be influenced by someone who is mature and uncompromised in the things of God. Father, we pray that you will cover all marriages with your precious blood. We pray Father, that you would shield them from all outside influences and meddling. Protect these marriages from every spirit that comes to kill, steal and destroy. (John 10v10) We bind the spirits of lying, lust, fornication, adultery, and every home wrecker spirit. We bind the spirit of compromise, seduction and temptation. And we pray Father, that you loose truth, loyalty, commitment, righteousness, faithfulness and the fear of God in the hearts of all spouses. Scripture says when a man finds a wife he finds a good thing and he obtains favor from the Lord. (Prov. 18v22) The scripture also says that man should leave his mother and father and cleave to his wife and the two shall become one. (Gen 2v24) The scripture also says it is not good for man to be alone. Father, we pray that you will go ahead of your unmarried children who desire marriage; and help them to be yoked up with the right partner. And Father your desire is for all to come to the saving grace of Christ Jesus. Father, your word even goes on to say what you have joined together let no man put asunder; for they are no longer two but one flesh. (Matt. 19v6). We pray a blessing over every marriage, over their finances, blessings over there health, blessings over their future, blessings over their children and families. Father, protect them from separation and divorce. Father, you said we have not because we asked not. Father we ask you these things in your son Jesus' name. Amen

Notes to Self

There is a Fountain
There is a fountain
Filled with blood
Drawn from Immanuel's veins
And sinners plunged beneath that blood
Lose all their guilty stains
Lose all their guilty stains
Lose all their guilty stains
And sinners plunged beneath that flood

Break Every Chain – see lyrics on line
(This song performed by American recording artist Tasha Cobbs)

Because He Lives – see lyrics on line
(Written by Bill and Gloria Gaither)

PRAYER FOR CHILDREN

Let us sing our 3 Worship songs to Usher us into the Presence of God:

There is a Fountain
Break Every Chain
Because He Lives

Prayer: Heavenly Father we come before your throne of grace today to say thank you. Thank you for salvation. Thank you for life, health, and strength. Thank you for your grace and mercy. Thank you for our eyes that see. Thank you for our ears that hear. Thank you for the blood running warm in our veins. Thank you for the roof over our head and the clothes on our back. Thank you for clean running water. Thank you that we're able to dress ourselves, and we're able to feed ourselves. Thank you for keeping my bodies healthy. All our organs are still operating at the level of perfection for which you commanded them to operate. Father, we don't take any of these blessings for granted. So, we bless your Holy name. Father, forgive us for sinning against you. We have sinned with our heart, we have sinned with our mouth and our hearts. Father, forgive us. Father, wash us, purge us, and cleanse us from all unrighteousness. (Psalms 51) Lord have mercy on us according to your loving kindness and according to your tender mercies. Father, you said if we ask for forgiveness that you would be faithful and just to forgive us from all unrighteousness. (1 John 1v9) Father we come today lifting up our children to you. We come lifting up the community children, the children that attend our church and even the children across this nation Oh God! We pray Father that you will be with our children. We pray Father that you would walk with them, that you would open their ears so that that can hear when you talk to them. We pray Father that you would lead them and guide them. We pray Father that you would protect them and cover them with your precious blood. We pray

Father that your angels would watch over them to take them safely over the highways and the byways and bring them back home safely. Father, your word tells us to train up a child in the way he should go and when he gets old that he wouldn't depart from it. (Prov. 22v6) Father, your word says that our children shall be taught of the Lord and great shall be there peace. (Isa 54v13) Father, your word says our children shall be like olive branches around about thy tables. (Psa. 128v3) Father, your word says our children shall not labor in vain, nor bring forth trouble; for they are the seed of the blessed of the Lord, and their offspring with them. (Isa 65v23) Father, your word says that you would establish thy covenant with us and with our descendants. (Gen6v18) Father, help us to teach our children your words, which can make them wise unto salvation thru faith in Christ. Father, God protect them from drugs and alcohol addictions. Father, keep them away from jails and prison cells. Father, keep them away from gang affiliations, stray bullets, drive by shootings, kidnappings, murders, rape and unwed pregnancy. Father, open their hearts and mind so that they will be able to discern wrong friendships wrong relationships. Father, protect the seed of your word that has been planted in them. Father, shield them, strengthen them, lead them and guide them. Help lead to find those people who are connected to their destinies. Father, help lead them to find those people that are travelling the same road of righteousness and holiness Oh God. Father, give them a mind to serve you early in life. Father, please hear our cry and attend unto our prayers. Father we can't do anything without you. Father, we are asking you all these things in your son Jesus' name. Amen

Notes to Self

Jesus Loves the Little Children
Jesus loves the little children
All the children of the world
Red, brown, yellow
Black and white
They are precious in His sight.
Jesus loves the little children
Of the world
Jesus died for all the children

Lord Prepare me to be a Sanctuary – see lyrics on line
(This song is performed by many artists)

I Love You Lord – see lyrics on line
(Performed by Laurie Klein)

PRAYER FOR REBELLIOUS

Let us sing our 3 Worship songs to Usher us into the Presence of God:

Jesus loves the Little Children
Lord Prepare Me to Be a Sanctuary
I love You Lord and I Lift My Voice

Prayer: Heavenly Father we come before your throne of grace today to say thank you. Thank you for life, health, and strength. Thank you for your grace and mercy. Thank you for the roof over our head and the clothes on our back. Thank you for the shoes on our feet. Thank you for clean running water. Thank you for never leaving and for never forsaking us. Thank you for being a very present help in the time of in trouble. (Psalm 46v1) Father, thank you! Father, we ask you to forgive us of our sins. Father, we know that we sin with our mouth, we sin with our hearts and we even sin in our mind. Father, we ask you to forgive us Lord! Father we need your help! Father, we pray and ask you to wash us, to purge us, to cleanse us from all unrighteousness. Father, you said if we asked for forgiveness that you would be faithful and just to forgive us and cleanse us from all unrighteousness. (1 John1v9) Father, we realize that we can do nothing apart from you. Father, we need you to go before us to make crooked places straight. Father, as you were with Moses we need you to be with us and our children. Father, we come today lifting up our disobedient children to you, Oh God. We come asking you to be with them wherever they are, be with them wherever they go. Father, we pray that you will circumcise their hearts and those who they are running with. We pray Father that you would deliver then from the power of darkness. We pray Father that you would send laborers across their paths. We pray Father that you will separate them from the wrong company that they are running with. We take authority over every spirit of drug and alcohol addiction, over every spirit of disrespect, dishonor, and every spirit of physical and verbal abuse and we bind it right now in the name of Jesus. We pray Father that you would loose self-control, respect and honor in the hearts and mind right now in our children in the name of Jesus. We pray Father that they would not come to the house intoxicated or drugged out of their minds. We pray Father that they would be respectable and kind to the other family members. We pray Father that you would cause the seed of your word to spring forth in their lives. Father, we pray that every plant that the heavenly father did not plan be rooted it out of their lives in the name of Jesus. Father, teach them the ways of your decrees that they may follow them to the end. Father, give them understanding that they may keep your law and obey it with all of their heart. (Psalms 119v33, 34) Father, help us to remain calm, in control, speaking in low tones and showing forth your love peace, and gentleness always. And more so when they show up at the house intoxicated. Father, help our children to understand that your heart and our hearts is filled with pain over sin, and yet you are gracious, slow to anger and abounding in love. (Psalms 103 v 8) Help us to remain in a spirit of patience, prayerfulness and meekness as we work with them to bring healing to their souls. Father give us, the parents/guardian wisdom for travelling this road with them for their complete healing deliverance. Father, we can do nothing if you don't intervene. Father, send help from the sanctuary. Father, send forth your ministering spirits to help us. Father, you said we have not because we have asked not. We need you now Jesus. In Jesus' name we pray. Amen

Notes to Self

Are You Washed in the Blood
Have you been to Jesus for the cleansing power?
Are you washed in the blood of the Lamb?
Are you fully trusting in His grace this hour?
Are you washed in the blood of the Lamb?

Are you washed in the blood?
In the soul cleansing blood of the Lamb?
Are your garments spotless, are they white as snow?
Are you washed in the blood of the Lamb?

Blessed Assurance – see lyrics on line
(This song is performed by many artists)

Precious Lord Take My Hand – see lyrics on line
(This song is performed by many artists)

PRAYING FOR THE PRESIDENT
& HIS CABINET MEMBERS

Let us sing our 3 Worship songs to Usher us into the Presence of God:

Are You Washed in the Blood
Blessed Assurance
Precious Lord Take My Hand

Prayer: Heavenly Father we come before your throne of Grace today to say thank you. Thank you for life, health and strength. Thank you for the blood running warm thru our veins. Thank you for the roof over our head. Thank you for the clothes on our backs and the shoes for our feet. Thank you for clean running water. Thank you for sending Jesus to die on the cross in our place. Father, we thank you that all our bills are paid, and all our needs are met. We thank you for our church family and our communities. Father, where would we be without you Oh God! Father, you allowed us to see this new day God and we dare not take it for granted. Father, we know that someone didn't wake up from their sleep Oh God. Father, we know someone woke up in a hospital room. Father, someone woke up from their sleep but couldn't get out of bed on their own. Lord you had mercy on us again and we say thank you. Father, please forgive us for our sins. We know we lie, steal and cheat and yet you continue to give us another chance. Father wash us, purge us, and cleanse us from all unrighteousness. Father, create in us a clean heart and renew a right spirit within us. (Psalms 51) Father, you said if we ask for forgiveness that you would be faithful and just to forgive us of all of our sin and to cleanse us of all unrighteousness. (1 John 1v9) Father, today we come to lift up the President and his cabinet members to you. Father, we lift up the cabinet members and their families and those that are assigned to work with them. We pray Father that you would bless them with Godly wisdom, understanding and knowledge.

Father, we pray that you would surround them with your angels. Father, we pray that you would surround them with the right people; those that love you Oh God. Father, surround them with those that believe in you and in your word as they make decisions for this great nation. Father, even as they legislate new laws lead them, guide them, instruct them. Father, give them the answers to difficult issues plaguing this nation. Father, teach them to saturate the atmosphere with your presence; singing and praising your Holy name before they even began to legislate. Father, for those that don't know you in the pardoning of their sin; we pray that they will desire to have a relationship with you. Father, we are praying for a new thing for this nation. Father, we pray that you will work in the heart of both parties for unity, revival and reconciliation. Father, scripture says you hold the kings heart in your hand and like streams of water you will turn it where you please. (Prov. 21v1) Father, we pray that the President and his cabinet members will cry out to you like Solomon and say give me your justice Oh God and your righteousness. Teach me to judge your people with righteousness and your poor with justice. Teach me how to defend the cause of the poor people and give deliverance to the children of the needy and to crush the oppressor. Father, help our leaders to lead your people and accomplish all that you please. (Isa 44v28) As we the people intercede for his success and the success of this nation. Father, hear our prayer oh God and attend unto our prayers. (Psalms 61 verse 1) Father, you said your ears are open to the cries of the righteous. Father help us! Father, there is nothing too hard for you. We are leaning and depending on you Oh God! It is in your son Jesus' name we pray. Amen

Notes to Self

Hear My Cry Oh' Lord
Hear my cry Oh Lord
Attend unto my prayers
From the ends of the earth,
Will I cry out to thee
When my heart is overwhelmed,
Lead me to the rock
That is higher than I
That is higher than I

Lord I Lift Your Name on High – see lyrics on line
(This song is performed by many artists)

My Jesus My Savior – see lyrics on line
(Written by Darlene Zschech)

PRAYER FOR UNITY AND PEACE

Let us sing our 3 Worship songs to Usher us into the Presence of God:

Hear My Cry Oh' Lord Attend unto My Prayer
Lord I Lift Your Name on High
My Jesus My Savior

Prayer: Heavenly Father we come before your throne of grace today to say thank you. Thank you for life, health, and strength. Thank you for your grace and mercy. Thank you for never leaving us and forsaking us. Thank you for our families. Thank you for the blood running warm in our veins. Thank you for the roof over our heads. Thank you for the clothes on back and the shoes for our feet. Father, we thank you for healthy bodies and sound minds. Father, we thank you for this new day that we have never seen before. Father, we thank you for never leaving us and never forsaking us. Father, we ask you to forgive us of our sins. Father, forgive us for sins of omission and our sins of commissions. Father, help us! Father, you said that if we ask for forgiveness that you would be faithful and just to forgive us of our sins and to cleanse us from all unrighteousness. (1 John 1v9) Father, we pray that you would create a clean heart in us and renew the right spirit. (Psalms 51) We need you God to lead us and guide us. We need you Father to go before us and make the crooked places straight. (Isa 45v2-4) Father, today we come lift up this nation for unity and peace. Father, we pray for unity and peace in your churches, we pray for unity and peace in the white house, we pray for unity and peace in every department of the government, we pray for unity in peace in our hearts and minds, we pray for unity and peace in our families, we pray for unity and peace in our community, we pray for unity and peace in every nation, we pray for unity and peace on every job. Oh, Father help us! Father, help us to look inside of ourselves first and take inventory of the condition of our hearts.

Help us to remember that you commanded us to forgive each other 70 x 7 times per day. (Matt 18v22) Father, you know that sometimes that this isn't always easy, so we pray God that you will forgive thru us. Father, we pray that you would teach us how to Agape love one another. Father, you said that you want us to be one just as you and the Father are one. (John 17v21) Father, help us to not only be hearers of your word but doers of your word. (James 1v22) Father, we pray that you would help us to remember that we are not a part of the world; that you have commanded us to come out of the world. (2 Corinth 6v17) Father, you commanded us be ye transformed by the renewing of your minds. (Rom 12v2) Father, help us to keep an upward gaze looking unto the hills from whence cometh our help; and helping us to discern the times. (Psalms 121v1,2) (Luke 12v54) Father, help us to gird up the loins of our minds, to be sober and hope to the end for the grace that is brought unto us at the revelation of Jesus Christ. (1 Pet 1v13) Father, we pray that you would help us to watch and pray, lest we enter in to temptation. Father, help us to cast all our cares on you because you care for us. Father, you said all thing are working for the good of them, those who love the Lord and who are called according to his purpose. (Rom 8v28) Father, help us to rest in you. Father, you said we have not because we ask not. We are asking now In Jesus' name. Amen

Notes to Self

Give to the Lord
Give and it will come back to you
Good measure pressed down, shaken together and
Running over
Give and it will come back to you
When you give, give to the Lord
Give and it will come back to you
Good measure pressed down, shaken together and
Running over

We're Blessed – see lyrics on line
(Written by Fred Hammond)

Thank You Lord – see lyrics on line
(Written by Paul Baloche)

PRAYER FOR FINANCES

Let us sing our 3 Worship songs to Usher us into the Presence of God:

Give to the Lord
We're Blessed
Thank You Lord

Prayer: Heavenly Father we come before your throne of grace today to say thank you. Thank you for life, health, and strength. Thank you for your grace and mercy. Thank you for the roof over our heads and the clothes on our backs. Thank you for the shoes on our feet. Thank you for clean running water. Thank you that all of our bills are paid, and all of our needs are met. Father, we thank you for being King of Kings and Lord of Lords. We thank you for being the lifter of our heads. We thank you for all things pertaining to life and goodliness, through the knowledge of him that hath called us to glory and virtue. (2 Pet 1v3) Father, we thank you for this new day that we've never seen before. Father, we commit this day into your hands. Father, we command this day will bring forward favor, promotion, increase, protection and every spiritual blessing. (Psalms 19v1-3) Father, you alone are good, you are holy, and you are righteous. Father, forgive us of our sins. Father, we pray that you will wash us, cleanse us, and purge us. Father, we pray that you will create in us a clean heart and renew a right spirit within us. (Psalms 51) Help us Oh God to not lift our souls unto vanity nor swear deceitfully. (Psalms 24v1-6) The scripture says for he shall receive the blessings from the Lord, and his righteousness is from the God of his salvation. This is the generation of them that seek him, that seek thy face, O Jacob. Selah. Father, we come to lift up our finances. Father, cause our finances to increase! Father, your word says that you wish above all that we may prosper and be in health even as our souls prospers. (3 John1v3) We pray Father that you would prosper us in every area of our lives. We pray for health, we pray for great marriages, for great social relationships, and we pray for great increase in our bank accounts. Father, help us to not be greedy or stingy. Father, you said if we give it will be returned unto us; good measure, pressed down, shaken together to make room for more and running over and poured into our lap. Father, we know the amount we give will determine the amount we get back. (Luke 6v38) Father, you commanded us to honor you with our wealth and the best part of everything we produce. Then you will fill our barns with grains and our vats will overflow with good wine. (Prov. 3v9,10) Father we pray that you will help us to remember to bring all our tithes into your storehouse so that there will be meet in the storehouse and if we do you will open the windows of heaven to pour us out a blessing that we don't have room enough to receive. (Mal. 3v8-10) Father, you said you would supply all my needs according to your riches in glory. (Phil. 4v19) Father, your word says that the blessing of the Lord maketh rich and adds no sorrow. (Prov. 10v22) Father, scripture says blessed are those who trust in the Lord and have made the Lord their hope and confidence. They will be like a tree planted by the waters that send out its root by the stream. It does not fear when heat comes it leaves are always green (Jere 17v7,8) and they have no worry during the year of drought and never fails to bear fruit. Father we remind you that you said that it is you who gives us the power to get wealth and so confirm your covenant. (Deut. 8v18) So, Father, we are reminding you of your word. Father, hear our cries, Oh Lord and attend unto our prayers. You said we have not because we ask not. We are asking you today in your son Jesus' name. Amen

Note to Self

Lord I Need You
Lord, I come, I confess
Bowing here I find my rest
Without You I fall apart
You're the One that guides my heart
Lord, I need You, oh, I need You
Every hour I need You
My one defense, my righteousness
Oh God, how I need You

Here I am to Worship – see lyrics on line
(This song is performed by many artists)

Holy Spirit Jesus Culture – see lyrics on line
(This song is performed by many artists)

Notes to Self

PRAYER FOR HEALING

Let us sing our 3 Worship songs to Usher us into the Presence of God:

Here I am to Worship
Lord I need You
Holy Spirit Jesus Culture

Prayer: Heavenly Father we come before your throne of grace today to say thank you. Thank you for life, health, and strength. Thank you for grace and mercy. Thank you for the blood running warm in our veins. Thank you for the roof over our heads. Thank you for the clothes on our back and the shoes for our feet. Father we thank you for clean running water. Father, we thank you for never leaving us and for never forsaking us. Thank you for keeping us in our right mind. Father, we thank you for the five senses you gave us. Father, we thank you for allowing us to see this new day that you have created. Father, we know that some where someone didn't make it into this new day. Father, we know that some where someone woke up in a hospital room. Father, we know some where some of us have loved ones incarcerated, and to remember those sick in the hospitals. Be with them today God. Father, we say thank you again for keeping us. Even as we slept and slumber on last night you watched over us Father. If we had 10,000 tongues, we couldn't praise or thank you enough. Father, we ask for your forgiveness. Forgive us for our sin. Father, we have sinned with our mind, we have sinned with our mouths and even without hearts. Help us God. We can't do anything without you. Father, wash us, purge us, cleanse us from all unrighteousness and create in us a clean heart and renew a right spirit within us. (Psalms 51) Father you said if we asked for forgiveness that you would be faithful and just to forgive us and cleanse us from all unrighteousness. (1 John 1v9) Father, today we come to lift up those that need a healing in their body. Father, touch us your people. Father, touch all blood conditions. Father, touch all cancer conditions. Father, touch all mind conditions. Father, touch all heart conditions. Father, heal us of every condition that Jesus' bore in his body when he received the 39 strips. Father, touch them from the crown of their heads to the soles of their feet. Father, make every organ new, make the blood cells new, cause the chemicals and the electrical impulses in the brain to work properly. Father, your word says that you were wounded for our transgressions and bruised for our iniquities and the chastisement of our peace was upon you and with your stripes we were healed. (Isa 53v5) Father, your word also says if there is any sick among you? Let them call for the elders of the church; and let them pray over him, anointing him with oil in the name of the Lord. And, the prayer of faith shall save the sick, and the Lord shall raise him up; and if he has committed any sins they shall forgive him. Confess your faults one to another and pray for one another that ye may be healed. The effectual fervent prayer of a righteous man availeth much. (James 5 v14-16) Father, we pray that we will live our lives according to your word so that our prayers not be hindered. Father, we thank you for bearing our diseases in your body on the tree. (1Pet 2v24) Father your word says that if we abide in your word and your word abide in us we can ask you what we and it will be done for us. (John 15v17) Father, your words said that your eyes are on the righteous and your ears are open to their prayers. (1 Pet 3v12) Father, we thank you for hearing our prayers. We ask you all these things in your son Jesus' name. Amen

I know it was the Blood

I know it was the blood,
I know it was the blood,
I know it was the blood for me
One day when I was lost, He died upon the cross
And I know it was the blood for me
(Repeat)

They pierced Him in the side
They pierced Him in the side
They pierced Him in the side for me

Set a Fire Down in my Soul – see lyrics on line
(Performed by various artists)

Holy Spirit – see lyrics on line
(Performed by various artists)

PRAYER FOR DELIVERANCE

Let us sing our 3 Worship songs to Usher us into the Presence of God:

I know it Was the Blood
Set a Fire Down in My Soul
Holy Spirit

Prayer: Heavenly Father we come before your throne of grace today to say thank you. Thank you for life, health, and strength. Thank you for your grace and mercy. Thank you for the roof over our head. Thank you for the clothes on our back and the shoes on our feet. Thank you for clean running water. Thank you that all our bills are paid, and all our needs are met. Thank you for the blood running warm in our veins. Thank you for allowing us to see another day. Thank you for watching over us as we slept and slumbered on last night. Father, we know that some where someone didn't make it to this new day. Father, we know some where someone woke up in a hospital bed. Father, some where someone woke and didn't have any food to eat. Father, someone woke up sleeping outside. Father, we thank you for taking care of us. And Father please remember those who are less fortunate than we are today. We pray that you will supply their needs according to your riches in glory through Christ Jesus. (Phillip 4v19) Father, we ask you to forgive us of our sins. Father, we know that we sin with our heart, we sin with our mind and we even sin with our tongue. Father, forgive us for our sins of omissions and our sins of commissions. Father, we ask you to wash us, purge us, cleanse us from all unrighteousness. Father, we pray that you create in us a clean heart and renew a right spirit within us. (Psalms 51) Father, we can do nothing without you. Father, we need you to lead us, to guide us, to instruct us, and to protect us. Father, we need you to change us, correct us and walk with us. Father, today we come praying for our deliverance. Father, help us to set our affection on things above, not on things of the earth. You said Father that we should mortify therefore our members which are upon the earth; fornication, uncleanness, inordinate affections, evil concupiscence, and covetousness, which is idolatry. For these things the wrath of God cometh upon the children of disobedience. Father you also said put off all of these anger, wrath, blasphemy, filthy communication out of you mouth. Lie not one to another, seeing that you have put off the old man and his deeds. (Colossians 3) Father, we come asking for help God. We pray Father for your divine intervention. Father, help us to walk in the Spirit so we don't fulfill the lust of the flesh. (Gal 5v16) Father, we renounce every evil, unrighteous, and ungodly spirit from our lives. Father, you are our Lord and Savior. You have given us the power and authority to allow and to disallow every work of darkness. Father, we pray that you would close every wrong door that we have opened in our lives. Father, we pray that you would open the right doors for us. Father, you said whatever we bind on earth that you would bind it in heaven. Father, we bind every spirit of lust, drunkenness, and drug addictions. We bind every spirit of anger, hatred, unforgiveness, depression and bitterness. Father you said whatever we loose on earth that you would loose in heaven. Father we pray that you would loose love, forgiveness, self control and commitment, loyalty, joy and peace and all your fruit in the name of Jesus. Also, we thank you for victory this day in the name of Jesus. (Matt 18v18) Father, we thank you for hearing our prayers. Father, we thank you because you said if we abide in your word and your word abide in us we can ask you what we will. Father, we ask you all these things in your son Jesus' name. Amen

Notes to Self

Amazing Grace
Amazing Grace, how sweet the sound
That saved a wretch like me
I once was lost, but now am found
T'was blind but now I see
T'was Grace that taught my heart to fear
And Grace, my fears relieved
How precious did that grace appear
The hour I first believed

10,000 Reasons – see lyrics on line
(co-written by Matt Redman and Jonas Myrin)

Here I am to Worship – see lyrics on line
(Performed by various artists)

PRAYER FOR THE LOST

Let us sing our 3 Worship songs to Usher us into the Presence of God:

Amazing Grace
10,000 Reasons
Here I am to Worship

Prayer: Heavenly Father we come before your throne of grace today to say thank you. Thank you for life, health, and strength. Thank you for your grace and mercy. Thank you for the roof over our head. Thank you for the clothes on our back and for the shoes on our feet. Thank you for clean running water. Thank you that all our bills are paid, and all of our needs are met. Thank you for never leaving us and for never forsaking us. Father, we thank you for the use of our limbs and the activity of our body. Father, we thank you for allowing us to see this new day. Father, we know that someone didn't wake up this morning. Father, we know that someone woke up in a hospital room. Father, someone woke up and didn't have any food to eat. Father, we pray that you even remember those that have lost loved ones, remember those that are in the hospital, remember those that don't have food. Father, we pray that you would meet the need of our neighbors near and far. Father, we ask that you forgive us of our sins. Father, we sin with our mouth, we sin with our minds, and we even sin with our hearts. Father, have mercy on us your people. Father, without you we can do nothing. Father, we pray that you would change our hearts and our minds. Help us to be more like you God. Father, you said if we asked for forgiveness that you would be faithful and just to forgive us of our sins and you would cleanse us from all unrighteousness. (1 John 1v9) Father, today we come to lift up our lost loved ones and our lost neighbors to you. Father, we come to lift up the hearts and minds of these people. Father, your word says no one can come to you except the Father who sent me draws them. (John 6v44) Father, we pray that you would quicken the hearts of those who are dead in sins and transgressions. (Eph. 2v1) Father, we pray that you would rebuke the God of this age who has blinded the minds of unbelievers. (2 Corin. 4v4) Father, we pray that you would open their hearts to hear the gospel and softened their calloused hearts. Father, remove from their minds any false teachings. (Act 16v14) Father, we pray that the fallow grounds of their hearts will be broken up so when the seed of the word come that it will fall on good ground take root and spring up. (Hosea 10v12) Father, remove the scales from their eyes. (Acts 9v18) Father, we pray that you would circumcise their hearts. Father, we pray that you would begin to speak to them as they lie on their bed. Father, we pray that you would speak to them while they are in the shower, speak to them as they drive in their car. Father, whatever it takes please don't let them die and go to hell. Father, you didn't create hell for people but for the fallen angels. As we know that the Lord isn't slow in fulfilling his promise, but is patient toward us, not wishing that any should perish but all should reach repentance. Father, you said every knee will bow and every tongue will confess Jesus as Lord. Father, put a hook in their jaw and draw them in. Father, help us to be wise as a serpent a harmless as a dove. (Matt 10v16) Father, you said he that win souls is wise. (Prov. 11v30) Father, we thank you for your ears are open to the prayers of the righteous. You said we have not because we ask not. We are asking you now in the name of Jesus' we pray. Amen

Notes to Self

I Need Thee
I need thee every hour
Most Gracious Lord;
No Tender voice like thine
Can peace afford.

I need thee, Oh I need thee
Every hour I need thee;
Oh, bless me now, my savior
I come to thee.

One Day at a Time – see lyrics on line
(written by Marijohn Wilkin and Kris Kristofferson)

Great is Thy Faithfulness – see lyrics on line
(Performed by various artists)

PRAYER FOR WISDOM

Let us sing our 3 Worship songs to Usher us into the Presence of God:

I Need Thee
One Day at a Time
Great is Thy Faithfulness

Prayer: Heavenly Father we come before your throne of grace today to say thank you. Thank you for life, health and strength. Thank you for your grace and mercy. Thank you for the roof over our head. Thank you for the clothes on our back and the shoes for our feet. Thank you for clean running water. Thank you for the blood running warm in our veins. Thank you for the use of our limbs and the activity in our body. Thank you for sending Jesus to die on Calvary in our place. We thank you for how you watched over us last night as we slept and slumbered. Father, we thank you for allowing us to see another day that we have never seen before. If we had 10,000 tongues, we couldn't tell you thank you enough. Father, we realize someone didn't wake up on this day. We realize someone woke up in a hospital room. Someone woke up sleeping under a bridge. Father, we owe you everything because you have been so good to us. Father, we now ask you to forgive us for our sins. Father, forgives us for our sins of omission and our sins of commission. Father, help us! Father, we sometime tell lies, steal and hold grudges. We know Father that we are a mess. Father, we acknowledge that we need you. Father, you said that if we asked for forgiveness that you would be faithful and just to forgive us and to cleanse us from all unrighteousness. (1 John1v9) Father, today we come praying for your wisdom. Your word said that if any man lacks wisdom that he can ask the Father who would give it liberally and will upbraided it not. (James 1v5) Father, we need you all the time. Father, we need wisdom on our jobs. Father, we need wisdom in our marriages. Father, we need wisdom while we are raising our families. Father, the scriptures says the teaching of the wise is a fountain of life, that one may turn away from the snares of death. (Prov. 13v14) Father, the scriptures say everyone who hears these words of mine and do them will be like a wise man who builds his house on the rocks. (Matt. 7v24) Father, you said to trust in the Lord with all thine heart and lean not to our own understanding in all thy ways acknowledge him and he would direct our path. (Prov. 3v5,6) Father, the scriptures says that Solomon loved you and that he walked in the statues of his father David, and that he made sacrifices and offerings at the high places. As did Solomon pray to God, that you have shown great and steadfast love to your servant David my father, because he walked before you in faithfulness, in righteousness and in uprightness of heart toward you. And you have kept for him this great and steadfast love and has given him a son to sit on his throne this day. Now, Oh Lord my God, you have made your servant king in place of David my father, although I am but a little child. I do not know how to go out or come in, and your servant is amid your people whom you have chosen, a great people, too many to be numbered or counted for multitude. Give your servant therefore an understanding mind to govern your people, that I may discern between good and evil, for who is able to govern this, your great people. (1 Kings 3v3-10) The scripture says you are not a respecter of person (Rom. 2v11) but, you are a respecter of faith. Father, hear our cry Oh God and attend to prayers today. (Psalms 61v1) Father, your ears are open to the prayer of the righteous. We ask you these things in the name of your son Jesus. Amen.

Notes to Self

What a Friend We Have in Jesus
What a Friend we have in Jesus, all our sins and griefs to bear!
What a privilege to carry everything to God in prayer!
O what peace we often forfeit, O what needless pain we bear,
All because we do not carry everything to God in prayer.

Have we trials and temptations? Is there trouble anywhere?
We should never be discouraged; take it to the Lord in prayer.
Can we find a friend so faithful who will all our sorrows share?
Jesus knows our every weakness; take it to the Lord in prayer.

Even in the Grave – see lyrics on line
(Performed by various artists)

I Will Do a New Thing in You – see lyrics on line
(Performed by various artists)

PRAYER FOR DEPRESSION

Let us sing our 3 Worship songs to Usher us into the Presence of God:

What a Friend We Have in Jesus
Even in the Grave
I Will Do a New Thing in You

Prayer: Heavenly Father we come before your throne of grace today to say thank you. Thank you for life, health, and strength. Thank you for your grace and your mercy. Thank you for the roof over our head. Thank you for the clothes on our back and the shoes for our feet. Thank you for clean running water. Thank you for all our bills are paid and all of our needs met. Father, we thank you for allowing us to see another day that we have never seen before. We thank you for the blood that continues to flow warm in our veins. Father, we thank you for another opportunity to tell someone about your saving grace. We thank you for sending Jesus to die on the cross in our place. Father, we ask that you forgive us for our sins. Father, forgive us for our sins of commission and our sins of omissions. Father, help us! Father, wash us, purge us, cleanse us from all unrighteousness and create in us a clean heart. Father, renew a right spirit within us. Father, wash us with the water of your word. As we say like Peter, not just my feet my hand, my head Lord and my whole body too. (John 13v8-10) You said if we ask for forgiveness that you would be faithful and just to forgive us for all sin and cleanse us from all unrighteousness. (1John1v9) Father, we come today to lift up those suffering with Depression. Father, the scripture say that you were wounded for our transgression that you were bruised for our iniquities and the chastisement of our peace was upon you and with your stripes we were healed. (Isa. 53v5) Father, you said that if we keep our mind on you that you would keep us in perfect peace. (Isa. 26v3) Father, your peace you leave us, your peace you give to us. You do not give to us as the world gives. Do not let our hearts be troubled and do not be afraid. (John 14v27) Father, help us to look up to you instead of looking elsewhere. Help us to magnify the name of Jesus rather than magnify the issues in our lives. Father, we pray that you would help us to meditate on your word when we are feeling down. Father, we pray that you help us to cast all our cares on you because you care for us. (1 Pet 5v7) Father, we pray that you would fill our mouth with songs of deliverance when we are down trodden. Father, your Word said to bless the Lord Oh my soul; and all that is within me, bless his holy name. Bless the Lord, Oh, my soul, and forget not all his benefits. Who forgiveth all thine iniquities, who healeth all thine disease; who redeemeth thy life from destruction, who crowneth thee with loving kindness and tender mercies, who satisfied thy mouth with good things; so that thy life is renewed like the eagle's. The Lord executeth righteousness and judgment for all that are oppressed. (Psalms 103v1-6) Father, you said that you would appoint unto them that mourn in Zion, to give unto them beauty for ashes, the oil of joy for mourning, the garment of praise for the spirit of heaviness, that they may be called trees of righteousness, the planting of the Lord, that he might be glorified. (Isa 61v3) Lord you are our strength and our shield; our heart trust in you and you helps us. (Psalms 28v7) The scripture says for I know the plans I have for you declares the Lord, plans to prosper you and not to hurt you, plans to give you a hope and a future. (Jerem. 29v11) Father, we thank you for healing and delivering us. We ask all these things in your son Jesus' name. Amen

Notes to Self

Standing on the Promises
Standing on the promises of Christ my King,
Through eternal ages let his praises ring;
Glory in the highest, I will shout and sing,
Standing on the promises of God.
Standing, standing,
Standing on the promises of God my Savior;
Standing, standing,
I'm standing on the promises of God.

Lord Prepare me – see lyrics on line
(written by Randy Lynn Scruggs)

Pass Me Not Oh Gentle Savior – see lyrics on line
(performed by various artists)

PRAYER FOR JOBS

Let us sing our 3 Worship songs to Usher us into the Presence of God:

Standing on the Promises
Lord Prepare Me
Pass Me Not Oh Gentle Savior

Prayer: Heavenly Father we come before your throne of grace today to say thank you. Thank you for life, health, and strength. Thank you for your grace and mercy. Thank you for the roof over our head. Thank you for the clothes on our back and the shoes for our feet. Thank you for clean running water. Thank you for the blood running warm in our veins. Thank you for the use and activity of our limbs. Thank you Jesus because we still have use of our eyes. Thank you for the ability to taste and smell. Thank you that we still have our sense of touch. We thank you for watching over us on last night as we slept and slumbered. Thank you for waking us up to see this new day. As we speak blessings into this day. We pray that this day will bring forth favor, prosperity, protection. We pray that this day will bring forth answered prayers. We pray this day will bring forth promotion and success. We pray this day will bring forth healing, reconciliation, and deliverance. We pray Father this day will bring forth opportunity to minister to the lost. Help us God to walk according to your Word. Father, we pray that you would forgive us for our sins. Forgive us for the sins of omission and for the sins of commissions. Father we pray that you forgive us for our anger, hatred and unforgiveness. Father, we pray that you forgive us for our lying, lust and stealing. Help us God! Father, you said that if we asked for forgiveness that you would be faithful and just to forgive us and heal us of all of sins and you would cleanse us from all unrighteousness. (1 John 1v9) Father, today we come praying for jobs for those that are unemployed. Father, you said in your Word that if we abide in your Word and your Word abide in us that we can ask you what we will and it shall be done for us. (John 15v7) Father, scripture says that if we take delight in your words that you would give me the desires of my heart. (Psalms 37v4) Father, we pray for job opportunities for all who are searching for employment. We pray God that your favor would be upon our names and our resumes. We pray that our resumes would stand out from all the others. We pray that you would touch the heart of the employer that his ears would be open to your voice, leading and guiding. We pray God that you would continue to supply seed to the sower and bread for food and you will also supply and increase your store of seed and enlarge the harvest of your righteousness. (2 Corinth 9v10) We thank you because you are our God and you said you would supply all our needs according to your riches in glory. (Phil. 4v19) Father, you said if we acknowledge you in all our ways that you would direct my paths. (Prov. 3v6) Father, we are coming to you because we are in need of jobs. You said that the earth is the Lord's and the fullness thereof, they and all that dwell therein. (Psalms 24v1) Father, we pray that you would move in this earth on our behalf. Father, you said that we are above and not beneath. You said the blessings Lord the blessing of the Lord maketh rich and add no sorrow. (Prov. 10v22) Father, you said we are blessed when we come in and blessed when we go out. (Deut. 28v1-13) Father, you said you would bless us and make us a blessing. (Gen 12v2) Father, we know that there is nothing too hard for you. (Jere 32v17) We pray God that you would hear our cry and attend unto our prayers. You said we have not because we ask not. We are asking you now Father in the name of Jesus we pray. Amen

Notes to Self

Are You Washed in the Blood of the Lamb
Have you been to Jesus for the cleansing power?
Are you washed in the blood of the Lamb?
Are you fully trusting in His grace this hour?
Are you washed in the blood of the Lamb?
Are you washed in the blood?
In the soul cleansing blood of the Lamb?
Are your garments spotless, are they white as snow?
Are you washed in the blood of the Lamb?

I Give Myself Away – see lyrics on line
(Written by Mike Oldfield)

My hope is Built on Nothing Less – see lyrics on line
(performed by various artists)

PRAYER FOR SCHOOLS

Let us sing our 3 Worship songs to Usher us into the Presence of God:

Are You Washed in the Blood of the Lamb
I Give Myself Away so You Can Use Me
My Hope is Built on Nothing Less

Prayer: Heavenly Father we come before your throne of grace today to say thank you. Thank you for life, health and strength. Thank you for your grace and mercy. Thank you for the roof over our head. Thank you for the clothes on our back and the shoes on our feet. Thank you for clean running water. Thank you that all our bills are paid, and all of our needs are met. Thank you for watching over us as we slept and slumbered on last night. Thank you for never leaving us and for never forsaking us. Thank you that the blood still flows warm in our veins. Thank you because we still have the use and activity of our limbs. Thank you for sending Jesus to die on the cross of Calvary for us. Father, we pray that you would forgive us for our sins; sins of omission as well as our sins of commission. We pray that you would forgive us for our anger, bitterness and unforgiveness. We pray that you would wash us, purge us, cleanse us with the water of your word. (Eph. 5v26) Father, you said that if we asked for forgiveness that you would be faithful and just to forgive us our sins and to cleanse us from all unrighteousness. (1 John 1v9) Father today we come to lift up the schools across the nation. We pray God that you place a hedge of protection around these schools Oh God! We pray that a hedge of protection would be around the children, those that work at the school and every visitor that enter these schools. We pray God that you would place the best teachers in these teaching positions. We pray that you place the right principals over our children, and over these schools Oh God, Father we pray like David from Psalms 23. The Lord is our shepherd; we shall not want. He maketh us to lie down in green pastures. He leadeth us by the still waters. He restored our soul. He leadeth us in a path of righteousness for his name's sake. Ye though we walked through the shadow of death we will fear no evil, for you are with us; your rod and staff comfort us. (Psalms 23v1-4) Father you are our God, our rock, in whom we take refuge, our shield; and the horn of our salvation, our stronghold and our refuge; our savior you save us from violence. Father, we pray against bullying, discrimination, sexual misconduct and harassment. Father, we pray for divine intervention in every situation. Father, you said to fear not for you are with us; be not dismayed; for you are your God, you will strengthen us, you will help us, you will uphold us with your righteous right hand. (Isa. 41v10) Father, your word said that no weapon formed against us shall prosper and every tongue risen against us in judgement we shall condemn. This is the heritage of the servant of the Lord and their righteousness is from me declares the Lord. (Isa 54v17) Father, we thank you because the scripture says that the Lord will keep us from all evil; he will keep our life. The Lord will keep our going out and our coming in from this time forth and forevermore. Father, we pray for your safety and protection in every classroom, in the cafeteria, in the hallways, in the administrative offices, in the nurse's lounge, the teachers' lounge, outside on the playgrounds, at the pool, even on the school buses as the children are being transported back and forth to and from schools. We pray Psalms 91 over every school across the land. We pray God that you would hear our cry Oh God and attend unto our prayers. We ask you all these things in Jesus' name we pray. Amen

Notes to Self

Count Your Blessings
When upon life's billows you are tempest tossed,
When you are discouraged, thinking all is lost,
Count your many blessings, name them one by one,
And it will surprise you what the Lord hath done.

Count your blessings, name them one by one;
Count your blessings, see what God hath done;
Count your blessings, name them one by one;
Count your many blessings, see what God hath done.

When We All Get to Heaven – see lyrics on line
(Written by Eliza Hewitt)

My Hope is Built on Nothing Less – see lyrics on line
(performed by various artists)

PRAYER FOR THE UNREACHED

Let us sing our 3 Worship songs to Usher us into the Presence of God:

Count Your Blessings
When We All Get to Heaven
My Hope is Built on Nothing Less

Prayer: Heavenly Father we come before your throne of grace today to say thank you. Thank you for life, health and strength. Thank you for your grace and mercy. Thank you for the roof over our head. Thank you for the clothes on our back and the shoes for our feet. Thank you for clean running water. We thank you that all our bills are paid. Thank you that all our needs are met. We thank you Father for never leaving us and for never forsaking us. We thank you for watching over us as we slept and slumbered. We thank you for allowing us to see this new day; this day that we have never seen before. Father, we realize that someone didn't wake up today. We realize God that someone woke up in a hospital room. We realize God that someone woke up today and don't have any food. We pray Father, that you would have mercy on those in every adverse situation. We pray God that you will meet there needs. We pray that you would turn their situations around and grant them a favorable outcome. Father, we pray that you would forgive us for our sins. We pray Father that you would wash us, purge us, and cleanse us from all unrighteousness. We pray that you will create in us a clean heart and renew the right spirit within us. (Psalms 51) Father, we pray that you would deliver us from anger, jealousy, and stealing, bitterness and hatred. We pray Father that you would remove the stony heart from us and give us a repenting heart of flesh. We pray Father that you would open our eyes and open our hearts. Father you said that if we asked for forgiveness that you would forgive us for our sins and that you would cleanse us from all unrighteousness. (1 John 1v9) Father, we need you God. We can't make it without you God. Father, we pray for those nations that don't know the name of Jesus. Father, scripture says how will they believe in him whom they have not heard, and how can they hear without a preacher. (Rom 10v14) We come to pray to the Lord of the harvest to send laborers; to every corner of the world proclaiming the name of Jesus. We pray for the reaping of the harvest; the harvest is plentiful, but the laborers are few. (Matt 9v37,38) We pray for every missionary that is partaker of harvest gathering. We pray God for their protection, we pray for them to have proper provision and for the hearts of the people to be receptive to the word of God. Father, we pray that they will have the necessary nourishments for the upkeep of their bodies. Father, give them favor over every nation that you would send them. Father, we thank you because the scripture says that after the Holy Ghost is come upon you; and you shall receive power, you will be witnesses to me in Jerusalem, and in all Judea and Samaria, and to the uttermost parts of the world. (Acts 1v8) Father, your words say that the Spirit of the Lord is upon me; because the Lord hath anointed me to preach good tidings unto the meek; he hath sent me to bind up the brokenhearted, to proclaim liberty to the captives, and the opening of the prison to them that are bound. (Isa 61v1) We pray that the word ministered would be mixed with faith so that the enemy does not come to immediately snatch it away. Father, protect, shield and fortify the investment of the seed of your word in the heart of these people. Father, unless you draw them they can't come bring them in Holy Spirit. You said we have not because we ask not. We are asking in Jesus' name. Amen

Notes to Self

Leaning on the Everlasting Arms
What a fellowship, what a joy divine,
Leaning on the everlasting arms;
What a blessedness, what a peace is mine,
Leaning on the everlasting arms.
Leaning, leaning,
Safe and secure from all alarms;
Leaning, leaning,
Leaning on the everlasting arms.

Shout to the Lord – see lyrics on line
(Performed by various artists)

To Worship You I Live – see lyrics on line
(Written by Israel Houghton)

PRAYER FOR EMERGENCY
RESPONSE TEAMS

Let us sing our 3 Worship songs to Usher us into the Presence of God:

Leaning on the Everlasting Arms
To Worship You I Live
Made a Way

Prayer: Heavenly Father we come before your throne of grace today to say thank you. Thank you for life, health, and strength. Thank you for your grace and mercy. Thank you for the roof over our head. Thank you for the clothes on our back and the shoes on our feet. Thank you for clean running water. Thank you that all our bills are paid, and all our needs are met. Father, we thank you for never leaving us and for never forsaking us. Thank you for the use of our limbs and activity of our body. Thank you, Father, for sending Jesus to die on Calvary's cross for us. Father, we pray that you would forgive us of our sins. Father forgive us for our sins of omission and commissions. Father, we know that we lie, steal and even cheat. Father, we realize that we can do nothing without you. Father, help us God! Father we cry out like David to you. We pray God that you would search our hearts and minds to see if there is any wicked way in us. Father, help us to lay aside every weight, and the sin that so easily beset us. (Heb. 12v1) Help us Father to love like you. Help us Father to forgive like you. Please go before us and make the crooked places straight. (Isa 45v2) Let him who means to love life and see good days refrain his tongue from evil and his lips from speaking guile, let him turn away from evil and do good; let him seek peace and pursue it. The eyes of the Lord are upon the righteous, and his ears attend to their prayers, but the face of the Lord is against those who do evil. (Psalms 34v10-12) Father, you said that if we ask for forgiveness that you would be faithful and just to forgive us and to cleanse us from all unrighteousness. (1 John 1v9) Father, we come today lifting up the Emergency Personnel Teams all across this nation. Father, these people hold dangerous jobs and they are putting their lives on the line for others every day. We pray a special prayer of protection over them Lord. We pray Psalms 91 over them. (Read it out loud) Father, your Word says that we can do all things through Christ who strengthens us. (Phil. 4v13) We pray that you will be their strength, and their courage. We pray that they will do the jobs assigned to them trusting and believing that you will never leave them, and you will never forsake them. Father. when they walk through the waters you will be with them, and when they pass through the rivers they will not sweep over them. When they walk through the fire, they will not be burned; the flames will not set them ablaze. (Isa. 43v2) Father, you said that you watch over you word to perform them. (Jerem. 1v12) You said just as the water comes down from heaven and waters the earth so does your word come down to accomplish and it does not return void (Isa 55v10). Father, we pray a hedge of protection around all of them. We pray for safety on every call that they will receive; because your angels are gone before them. Father, bless them with the best equipment. Bless them with peace, laughter and love. We pray against premature death. We pray against any sickness or disease. We pray blessings over every station and also their family members. Father hear our cry Oh Lord and attend to our Prayers. You said we have not because we asked not. Father we asking you right now in Jesus' name. Amen

Note to Self

Trust and Obey
When we walk with the Lord
In the light of His Word,
What a glory He sheds on our way;
While we do His good will,
He abides with us still,
And with all who will trust and obey. Trust and obey,
For there's no other way
To be happy in Jesus,

Victory Belongs to Jesus – see lyrics on line
(Created by Todd Dulaney)

You Deserve It – see lyrics on line
(by J.J. Hairston & Youthful Praise feat. Bishop Cortez Vaughn)

PRAYER FOR LOCAL SPIRITUAL LEADERS

Let us sing our 3 Worship songs to Usher us into the Presence of God:

Trust and Obey
Victory Belongs to Jesus
You Deserve It

Prayer: Heavenly Father we come before your throne of grace today to say thank you. Thank you for life, health, and strength. Thank you for your grace and mercy. Thank you for the roof over our heads. Thank you for the clothes on our back and the shoes for our feet. We thank you Father for clean running water. We thank you for the blood running warm in our veins. We thank you Father for the use of our limbs and the activity in our body. We thank you for never leaving us and for never forsaking us. We thank you for sending Jesus to die on Calvary cross in our stead. Father, we pray that you would forgive us of our sins. We pray for deliverance from our sins of omission and even sins of commissions. Father, we repent for lying, stealing and cheating. Father, we repent for anger, bitterness and unforgiveness. We can't make it without you God. Father, you said if we ask for forgiveness that you would be faithful and just to forgive us of our sins. You said that you cleanse us from all unrighteousness. (1 John 1v9) Father, help us we need you. Father, we need you to heal our nation, we need you to heal our government, we need you to heal our cities, our communities, we need you Father to heal our families. Father, we need you to heal our churches, and to heal our bodies Oh God. Father today we come lifting up churches all across the land. Father, we lift up the Prophets, Apostles, Pastors, the Evangelist and we lift up the teachers and all others in their respectable places. Father, we come as humble as we know how asking for your guidance Oh Father. We are praying Father, that we would begin to die to selfishness, die to wrong desires and wrong motives. Father, we realize that we have walked contrary to your word. Father, we realize that we haven't followed your leading. We realize Oh God that we have strayed from your truths, your word of truth. Father, we have not confronted sin in our camps. (Joshua 7v1-26). Father, we will no longer turn our heads and look the other way when sin encroaches. Father, forgive us for not being the leaders you have called us to be. Forgive us for being so distracted by things that aren't important to you. Father, forgive us for not properly caring for and nurturing your sheep. Father, forgive us for putting our own agendas ahead of your agenda. Father, help us to lead according to your word. Father, help us to teach your uncompromising word; and then the masses will come. Father, we pray as Solomon prayed. As Solomon said, you have shown us your great and steadfast love to your servant David my father, because he walked in your faithfulness and in your righteousness, and in uprightness of heart toward you. Still you have kept for him this great and steadfast love. You have given him a son to sit on his throne this day. Lord my God, you have made your servant king in place of David my Father, although I am but a little child. Father, we don't not how to go out or come in. Your servant is amid your people whom you have chosen, a great people, too many to be numbered or counted for a multitude. Therefore, give your servant an understanding mind to govern your people. That I may know good from evil for who is able to govern this great your people. Father, bring back your Glory to your tabernacle! Father, hear our cry today and attend unto our Prayers. In Jesus' Name we pray. Amen

Notes to Self

Love Lifted me
I was sinking deep in sin,
Far from the peaceful shore,
Very deeply stained within,
Sinking to rise no more.
But the Master of the sea
Heard my despairing cry,
From the waters lifted me.
Now safe am I.

Ancient of Days – see lyrics on line
(Performed by various artists)

Higher Place of Praise – see lyrics on line
(Performed by various artists)

PRAYER FOR SPOUSE

Let us sing our 3 Worship songs to Usher us into the Presence of God:

Love Lifted Me
Ancient of Days
Higher Place of Praise

Prayer: Heavenly Father we come before your throne of grace today to say thank you. Thank you for life, health and strength, for never leaving us or never forsaking us. Thank you for your grace and mercy, for never leaving us or never forsaking us. Thank you for the roof over our head. Thank you for the clothes on our back and the shoes for our feet. Thank you for clean running water. Father, we thank for watching over us as we slept and slumbered on last night. Thank you for waking us up in our right minds. Thank you for the use of our limbs and the activity of our body. Thank you for never leaving us and for never forsaking us. Father, you have been so good to us; better then we know how to be to ourselves. Father, we pray that you would forgive us of our sins. Father, forgive and deliver us for sins of omissions and our sins of commissions. Father, forgive us for anger, hatred and unforgiveness. Father, forgive us even for our secret sins; those sins that we think are hidden from you. Father, you said that if we ask for forgiveness that you would be faithful and just to forgive us and to cleanse us from all unrighteousness. (1 John 1v9) Father, we pray that you would wash us, purge us and create in us clean hands and a pure heart. (Psalms 51) Father, today we come lifting up to you our spouses. We thank you for blessing us with such a wonderful gift from above. We thank you because we understand the covenant that we made with our spouse and, with you God. We thank you for helping us to understand that this covenant is binding and living in your sight God. Help us to not to cross the line to break marital bonds. We thank you that we are walking together in agreement. (Amos 3v3) We thank you Father for teaching us how to love, cherish, respect and honor one another. Father, we thank you because your word says when a man finds a wife he finds a good thing and obtains favor from the Lord. (Prov. 18v22) Father, we thank you because your word says that the man shall leave his father and mother and be joined to his wife and the two shall become one flesh. (Gen 2v24) The scriptures also say what God has joined together let no man put asunder. (Mark 10v9) Father, we realize that our salvation is closer now than we first believed. Father, deliver us from the powers of darkness, help us to put on Christ Jesus daily. Father, helps us to not become ensnared by the lust of the flesh, the lust of the eyes and the pride of life. (John 2v16) Father, cause us to turn our eyes from worthless things, come to their sense to escape from the trap of the devil, who has taken them captives to do his will. (2 Timothy 2 v 26) Father, create a hunger and thirst for righteousness in our heart. Father, help us to find the calling you have predestinated for us. (Romans 8v30) Father, help us to meditate on your Word day and night so our ways will be prosperous. (Josh. 1v8) Help us to write your words on the table of our hearts so we don't sin against you. (Prov. 7v3) Father help us to not just be hearers of your word but doers also. (Jam. 1v22) Father we pray that you will cover our marriages with your precious blood. Father, we pray that you would grant unto us a double portion of your anointing of forgiveness. Help us to compromise and sacrifice our desires for the other. Father, send the right friends into our lives. Save and deliver us from those sins that we struggle with. Help us to keep our eyes on you. Help us to continually look up to you for our answers, for our guidance and for patience. Father, we need you; help us God. In Jesus' Name we pray. Amen

Notes to Self

Pass Me Not Oh Gentle Savior
Pass me not, Oh Gentle Savior
Hera my humble cry,
While on Others, Thou art calling
Do not pass me by.

Savior, Savior
Hear my humble cry
While on others, Thou art calling
Do not pass me by

Oh Come Let Us Adore Him – see lyrics on line
(Performed by various artists)

Worthy is the Lamb – see lyrics on line
(Written by Darlene Zschech)

PRAYER FOR ADDICTIONS

Let us sing our 3 Worship songs to Usher us into the Presence of God:

Pass Me Not Oh Gentle Savior
Oh, Come Let Us Adore him
Worthy is the Lamb

Prayer: Heavenly Father we come before your throne of grace today to say thank you. Thank you for life, health, and strength. Thank you for your grace and mercy. Thank you for the roof over our head. Thank you for the clothes on our back and the shoes for our feet. Thank you for clean running water. Thank you that all our bills are paid, and all our needs are met. We thank you for never leaving us and never forsaking us. Thank you for the blood running warm in our veins. Thank you for the use of our limbs and the activity in our body. Father, we realize that we can do nothing apart from you. Father, we realize that someone didn't wake up from their sleep today. Father, we realize that someone woke up in a hospital bed. We realize that someone can't feed their children. Father, we pray that you would meet the need of those who are dealing with adverse situations today. We pray that you would bless and strengthen them. We pray that you would bless them with good health, bless them with finances, and bless those families that may be dealing with bereavement. Father, we need you Oh God. Father, we ask that you forgive us for our sins; our sins of omission and, our sins of commissions. Father, we sometimes tell lies, sometimes we hold unforgiveness and bitterness. Oh God help us Jesus. We pray you would wash us, purge us, cleanse us from all unrighteousness and create a clean heart and renew the right spirit within us. (Psalms 51) Father, you said that if we were faithful and just that you would forgive us and cleanse us from all unrighteousness. (1 John 1v9) Father, today we come lifting up those who are struggling with addictions, to you.

Those who are battling addictions of alcoholism, drugs addictions, eating addictions, gambling addictions, sex addictions and so many others. We are calling on the name of Jesus today on their behalf. Father, help us, revive us and restore us according to your tender mercies and your loving kindness. Father, break us free from the powers of darkness. Father, your word said that for this reason was the son of God made manifest that he would destroy the works of darkness. (1 John 3v8) Father, break the powers of the enemy that have us in bondage. Father, you said if we call on the name of Jesus we shall be saved. (Rom. 10v13) Father, you also said at the name of Jesus every knee would bow (Phil. 2v10) so we command the knee of drug addiction to bow, we command the knee of alcoholism to bow, we command the knee of gambling to bow, we command the knee of overeating to bow, we command the knee of sexual sins to bow. We pray let God arise and his enemies be scattered. (Psalms 68v1) We command the enemy of drug addiction to scatter, the enemy of alcoholism to scatter, the enemy of gambling and overeating we command you to scatter. Thank you for giving us victory Father. Thank you for giving our family members victory. Thank you for giving those who are struggling victory as well. Thank you for our deliverance Father. Father, we pray that you would send ministering spirits to help us. (Heb. 1v14) Father, we pray that you would send help from the sanctuary. Father, you said we are surrounded by such a great cloud of witnesses. (Heb. 12v1) Father send the right people in our lives to help us on this recovery journey. Father, you said we have not because we ask not. We are asking today in Jesus' name. Amen.

Notes to Self

Jesus Paid It All
I hear the savior say, thy strength indeed is small
Child of weakness, watch and pray, find in me thine all in all
'Cause Jesus paid it all
All to him I owe
Sin had left a crimson stain, he washed it white as snow
Lord, now indeed I find thy power and thine alone
Can change the leper's spots and melt the heart of stone
'Cause Jesus paid it all

Take Me to the King – see lyrics on line
(Written by Kirk Franklin, performed by Tamela Mann)

Nobody Greater – see lyrics on line
(Written by Darius Paulk)

PRAYERS FOR SLEEPLESSNESS

Let us sing our 3 Worship songs to Usher us into the Presence of God:

Take Me to the King
Jesus Paid It All
Nobody Greater

Prayer: Heavenly Father we come before your throne of grace today to say thank you. Thank you for life, health and strength. Thank you for your grace and mercy. Thank you for never leaving me and never forsaking me. Thank you for being the lifter of my head. Thank you for the roof over our head. Thank you for the clothes on our back and the shoes for our feet. Thank you for clean running water. Thank you that all our bills are paid, and all our needs are met. Thank you for watching over us on last night as we slept and slumbered. Thank you for allowing us to see this new day. Father, we realize that someone somewhere didn't wake up to day. Father, we realize that someone woke up this morning in a hospital bed. Father, we realize someone woke up this morning and couldn't feed their children. Father, we pray and ask you to meet the needs of these people who are dealing with adverse situations today. Father, we pray that you would comfort the bereaving family, heal the body of that one in the hospital, and provide finance to that one that need food for their children. Father, we ask you to forgive us of our sins. Father, forgive us for our sins of omission as well as our sins of commissions. Father, we pray that you would wash us, purge us, and cleanse of all unrighteousness create in us clean hands and a pure heart. (Psalms 51) Father, you said that if we ask for forgiveness that you would be faithful and just to forgive us and to heal us from all unrighteousness. (1 John 1v9) Father, we come today lifting up those who are suffering from sleep deprivation and sleeping conditions. Father, we know that there is nothing too hard for you. Father, we come asking you to help us and to deliver us from all sleep disturbances. Hear me when I call, Oh God of my righteousness: thou hast enlarged me when I was in distress; have mercy upon me and hear my prayer. Oh, ye sons of men, how long will ye turn my glory into shame, but know that the Lord has set apart him that is Godly for himself: The Lord will hear when I call unto him. Stand in awe, and sin not: commune with your own heart upon your bed and be still. Selah. Offer the sacrifices of righteousness and put your trust in the Lord. Lord, lift thou up the light of thy countenance upon us. Thou hast put gladness in my heart, more than in the time that their corn and their wine increased. I will both lay me down in peace, and sleep; for thou, Lord, only makest me dwell in safety. (Psalms 4v1-8) Father, we say thank you. Father, we say thank you because your word say when thou liest down, thou shall not be afraid; yea, thou shalt lie down, and thou sleep shall be sweet. (Prov. 3v24) Your word says I laid me down and slept, thou awaked; for the Lord sustained me. (Psalms 3v5) Father, your word says that if we keep our minds on thee that you would keep us in perfect peace. (Isa 26v3) Father, we thank you for your power and authority of the works of darkness. Father, right now in the name of Jesus we bind the spirit of insomnia, the spirit of fear, the spirit of worry and any other spirit that is associated with this restless spirit. For it is written in Matthew 18v18 whatever we bind on earth is also bound in heaven. Father, right now we lose peaceful sound, undisturbed sleep. We decree victory over every agent of the enemy who comes to steal or break our sleep. We praise you Father for victory right now. Thank you for hearing our prayers. In Jesus' name. Amen

Notes to Self

Room at the Cross
There's room at the cross for you
There's room at the cross for you
Though millions have come
There's still room for one
Yes, there's room at the cross for you

There's room at the cross for you
There's room at the cross for you
Though millions have come

Fill Me Up – see lyrics on line
(Performed by Various Artists)

You Deserve the Glory – see lyrics on line
(Performed by Various Artists)

PRAYER FOR SPIRITUAL GROWTH

Let us sing our 3 Worship songs to Usher us into the Presence of God:

Room at the Cross
Fill Me Up
You Deserve the Glory

Prayer: Heavenly Father we come before your throne of grace today to say thank you. Thank you for life, health, and strength. Thank you for your grace and mercy. Thank you for the roof over our head. Thank you for the clothes on our back and the shoes for our feet. Thank you for clean running water. Thank you that all our bills are paid, and all our needs are met. We thank you for never leaving us and never forsaking us. Thank you for the blood running warm in our veins. Thank you for the use of our limbs and the activity in our body. Father, we realize that we can do nothing apart from you. Father, we realize that someone didn't wake up from their sleep. Father, we realize that someone woke up in a hospital bed. We realize that someone can't feed their children. Father we pray that you would meet there needs. We pray that you would bless them in their health, bless them with finances, and bless those families that may be dealing with bereavement. Father, we ask that you forgive us for our sins; our sins of omission and our sins of commissions. Father you words said that you are faithful and just that you would forgive us and cleanse us from all unrighteousness. (1 John 1 v 9) Father, today we come lifting up to you those who are seeking to draw closer to you. Father, we pray that you would remove every hindrance and every distraction from our lives. Father, your words says draw nigh to me and I will draw nigh to you. (James 4v8) The scripture says in (Jer. 31v3) Ye I have loved thee with an everlasting love: therefore, with loving kindness have I drawn thee. Father, help us to realize that drawing closer to you means spending time with you, reading your word more. Father, cultivate that desire in us and remove anything that's pulling us in the opposite direction. Father, help us to engage in worship daily with you; and our worship will draw us closer to you. Father, help us to desire your word more than our necessary food. (Job23v12) Father help us to realize that in order for us to draw closer to you that we will have to become more obedient to your word. Father help us to say like David I will bless the Lord at all times and his praise shall continually be in my mouth. My soul shall make her boast in the Lord; the humble shall hear thereof and be glad. O magnify the Lord with me and let us exalt his name together. I sought the Lord and he heard me. (Psalms 34v1-4) Therefore, since we have a great high priest who has gone through the heavens, Jesus the son of God, let us hold firmly to the faith we profess, for we do not have a high priest who is unable to sympathize with our weakness, but we have one who has been tempted in every way, just as we are-but is without sin. Let us then approach the throne of grace with confidence, so that we may receive mercy and find grace to help in our time of need. (Heb. 4v14-16). Father, we thank you for your ears being open to the prayers of the righteous. We ask you these things in Jesus' name. Amen

Notes to Self

There is a Name I Love to Hear
There is a name I love to hear
I love to sing its worth
It sounds like music in my ear
The sweetest name on Earth

Oh, how I love Jesus
Oh, how I love Jesus
Oh, how I love Jesus
Because he first loves me!

Nobody Like You Lord – see lyrics on line
(Written by Maranda Willis)

For Your Glory – see lyrics on line
(Performed by various performers)

PRAYERS FOR MOTHERS

Let us sing our 3 Worship songs to Usher us into the Presence of God:

There is a Name I Love to Hear
Nobody Like You Lord
For Your Glory

Prayer: Heavenly Father we come before your throne of grace today to say thank you. Thank you for life, health and strength. Thank you for your grace and mercy. Thank you for never leaving us and never forsaking us. Thank you for being the lifter of our head. Thank you for the roof over our head. Thank you for the clothes on our back and the shoes for our feet. Thank you for clean running water. Thank you that all our bills are paid, and all our needs are met. Thank you for watching over us on last night as we slept and slumbered. Thank you for allowing us to see this new day. Father, we realize that someone somewhere didn't wake up to day. Father, we realize that someone woke up this morning in a hospital bed. Father, we realize someone woke up this morning and couldn't feed their children. Father, we pray and ask you to meet the needs of these people who are dealing with adverse situations today. Father, we pray that you would comfort the bereaving family, heal the body of that one in the hospital, and provide finances to that one that need food for their children. We ask you, Father, to forgive us of our sins. Father, forgive us for our sins of omission as well as our sins of commissions. Father, we pray that you would wash us, purge us, and cleanse of all unrighteousness create in us clean hands and a pure heart. (Psalms 51) Father, you said that if we ask for forgiveness you would be faithful and just to forgive us; and to heal us from all unrighteousness. (1 John 1v9) Father we come today lifting up mothers all across the land. Father, we pray for your strength, wisdom, and for your guidance. We pray Father that you would bless them with wisdom, knowledge and understanding. Father, we pray for every mother, whether they are saved or unsaved, we pray for the educated and the uneducated, we are praying for the rich and the poor, we are praying for the sick and the well, we are praying for those in the states and those around the world, we are praying Father for your divine intervention. Father, we are praying that you would teach them, guide them, protect them, provide for them, heal them and restore them and their families. We pray Father that all mothers would come to know you. We pray Father that they will know you in the power of your resurrection and the fellowship of your suffering; becoming like you even unto death. (Phil. 3v10) Father, help us to be quick to hear and slow to speak. (James 1v9) Father, we pray that you would help us to be of a meek and quiet spirit. (1 Pet 3v4) Father, help us to find their strength in the truth of your Word Oh God. Father, help us to lead by example. Father, help us to weed out all ungodly contaminations seeking to attach themselves to their children. Father, help us to seek out those who can help us to mold them, shape them, encourage them, correct them, and instruct them in the things that are right and Godly in your sight. Father, help us to display that God-fearing spirit, a person of uprightness, holiness and compassion towards her family and all around them. Father, scripture says that we should teach a child in the way he should go so as when he gets old he will not depart from it. (Prov. 22v6) Father, we can do nothing without you. Father, you said we have not because we ask not. We are asking you all these things right now in the mighty name of Jesus. Amen

Notes to Self

We are Marching Up to Zion
Come ye that love the Lord, and let your joys be known,
Join in a song with sweet accord, Join in a song with sweet accord.
And thus surround the throne, and thus surround the throne.
We're marching to Zion, beautiful, beautiful Zion;
We're marching upward to Zion; the beautiful city of God
Then let our songs a bound and every tear be dry;
We're marching through Immanuel's ground; we're marching through
Immanuel's
Ground,

Never Would Have Made It – see lyrics on line
(Written by Matthew Brownie, Marvin Sapp)

Praise Him in Advance – see lyrics on line
(Written by Marvin Sapp)

PRAYERS FOR FATHERS

Let us sing our 3 Worship songs to Usher us into the Presence of God:

We Are Marching Up to Zion
Never Would Have Made It
Praise Him in Advance

Prayer: Heavenly Father we come before your throne of grace today to say thank you. Thank you for life, health, and strength. Thank you for your grace and mercy. Thank you for the roof over our head. Thank you for the clothes on our back and the shoes for our feet. Thank you for clean running water. Thank you that all our bills are paid, and all our needs are met. We thank you for never leaving us and never forsaking us. Thank you for the blood running warm in our veins. Thank you for the use of our limbs and the activity in our body. Father, we realize that we can do nothing apart from you. Father we realize that someone didn't wake up from their sleep today. Father, we realize that someone woke up in a hospital bed. We realize that someone can't feed their children today. Father we pray that you would meet the need of those who are dealing with adverse situations everywhere. We pray that you would meet every need for them. We pray that you would bless them in their health, bless them with finances, and bless those families that may be dealing with bereavement. Father, we need you Oh God. Father, we ask that you forgive us for our sins; our sins of omission and also our sins of commissions. Father, we sometimes tell lies, we hold unforgiveness and we steal. We pray you would wash us, purge us, cleanse us from all unrighteousness and create a clean heart and renew the right spirit within us. (Psalms 51) Father, you said that if we were faithful and just that you would forgive us and cleanse us from all unrighteousness. (1 John 1v9) Father, today we come lifting up to you all Fathers. We pray for the young and the old, the single and the married, the educated and the uneducated, the rich and the poor, the saved and the unsaved, those who left and those who stayed, those near and those who are far away, those in the states and those elsewhere around the world. Father, help them to weed out all ungodly contaminations seeking to attach themselves to our children. Father, help us to seek out those who can help us to mold them, shape them, encourage them, correct them, and instruct them in the things that are right and Godly in your sight. Father, we pray that you write your words on the tablet of our hearts. Father, scripture says in (Deut. 6v6-9) These commandments that I give you today are to be on your heart. Impress them on your children. Talk about them when you sit at home and talk about them when you walk along the road, when you lie down and when you get up. Tie them as symbols on your hand and bind them on your forehead. Father, write them on the doorframes of your house; and write them on your gates. The scripture says if serving the Lord seems undesirable then choose for yourself this day whom you will serve whether the Gods your ancestors served beyond the Euphrates, or the Gods of the Amorites, in whose land you are living. But as for me and my household, we will serve the Lord. (Josh 24v15) Father, scripture says that we should train up a child in the way he should go and when he gets old he will not depart from it. (Prov. 22v6) Father, we realize that we can do nothing without you. Father, you said we have not because we ask not. We ask you today to grant us all these things in Jesus' name. Amen.

Notes to Self

Revive Us Again
We praise Thee, O God,
For the Son of Thy love,
For our Savior who died and
Is now gone above. Hallelujah! Thine the glory,
Hallelujah! Amen;
Hallelujah! Thine the glory,
We praise Thee again.
We praise Thee, O God,

Firm Foundation – see lyrics on line
(Various Performers)

In Christ Alone – see lyrics on line
(There are two versions of this song)

PRAYER FOR MY OWN BUSINESS

Let us sing our 3 Worship songs to Usher us into the Presence of God:

Revive Us Again
Firm Foundation
In Christ Alone

Prayer: Heavenly Father we come before your throne of grace today to say thank you. Thank you for life, health, and strength. Thank you for your grace and mercy. Thank you for the roof over our head. Thank you for the clothes on our back and the shoes for our feet. Thank you for clean running water. Thank you that all our bills are paid, and all our needs are met. We thank you for never leaving us and never forsaking us. Thank you for the blood running warm in our veins. Thank you for the use of our limbs and the activity in our body. Father, we realize that we can nothing apart from you. Father, we realize that someone didn't wake up from their sleep today. Father, we realize that someone woke up in a hospital bed. We realize that someone can't feed their children. Father, we pray that you would meet the need of those who are dealing with adverse situations today. We pray that you would meet every need for them. We pray that you would bless them in the health, bless them with finances, and bless those families that may be dealing with bereavement. Father we need you. Father, we ask that you forgive us for our sins; our sins of omission and also our sins of commissions. Father, we sometimes tell lies, sometimes we hold unforgiveness and we are bitter. We pray you would wash us, purge us, cleanse us from all unrighteousness and create a clean heart and renew the right spirit within us. (Psalms 51) Father, you said that if we were faithful and just that you would forgive us and cleanse us from all unrighteousness. (1 John 1v9) Father, today we come lifting up to you those who are seeking their own business. We pray God for the proper connections. We pray for favor and open doors for our own business. Father, we pray that you send the proper mentor to help us to reach our desired destination. Father, send someone that won't mind our shadowing their behavior for us to reach that place of owning our own business. Father, your word said that you wished above all things that thou mayest prosper and be in good health even as thy soul prospers. (3 John 1v2) Father, you said I am the head and not the tail. I am above and not beneath. Father, you said I am the lender and the borrower. You said you would bless me and make me a blessing. (Deut. 28) Father, we pray that you would lead us, guide us, and instruct us in all that we do. Father, help us to prepare for the birth of our own business. Father, fill us with your wisdom, fill us with your knowledge, and your understanding. Father, you said for us to lean not to our own understanding but in all our ways to acknowledge you and you would direct our paths. (Prov. 3v5,6) Father, thank you because you said that your eyes are over their righteous and your ears are open to their prayers. (Psalms 34v15) Father, we pray like Jabez (1 Chron 4v10) that you would bless me indeed and enlarge my territory, that your hand would be with me, and that you would keep me from all evil, that I may cause no pain. Father, grant unto us the desire of our hearts. Father, you said when we give our tithes that you would open up the windows of heaven and pour out a blessing that we don't have room enough to receive. (Malachi 3v9,10) Father, you said if we abide in your word and your word abide in us that we can ask what we will and it will be done by the Father in heaven. (John 15v7) Father, you said we have not because we ask not. Father, we are asking in the name of your son Jesus. Amen

Notes to Self

Jesus Keep Me Near the Cross
Jesus, keep me near the cross,
There a precious fountain—
Free to all, a healing stream—
Flows from Calv'ry's mountain.
In the cross, in the cross,
Be my glory ever;
Till my raptured soul shall find
Rest beyond the river.

Something About the Name of Jesus – see lyrics on line
(Various Performers)

You Have Won the Victory – see lyrics on line
(Various Performers)

PRAYING FOR OUR ENEMY

Let us sing our 3 Worship songs to Usher us into the Presence of God:

Jesus Keep Me Near the Cross
Something About the Name of Jesus
You Have Won the Victory

Prayer: Heavenly Father we come before your throne of grace today to say thank you. Thank you for life, health, and strength. Thank you for your grace and mercy. Thank you for the roof over our head. Thank you for the clothes on our back and the shoes on our feet. Thank you for clean running water. Thank you that all our bills are paid, and all our needs are met. Father we thank you for never leaving us and for never forsaking us. Thank you for the use of our limbs and activity of our body. Thank you, Father, for sending Jesus to die on Calvary's cross for us. Father, we pray that you would forgive us of our sins. Father, forgive us for our sins of omission and our sins of commissions. Father we know that we lie, steal and even cheat. Father, we realize that we can do nothing without you. Father, help us Oh God! Father, we cry out like David to you Oh God. We pray God that you would search our hearts and minds to see if there is any wicked way in us. Father, if you find anything that isn't pleasing to you God we pray that you would perform a spiritual surgery on us Oh God. Father, help us to lay aside every weight, and the sin that so easily beset us. (Heb. 12v1) Help us Father to love like you. Help us Father to forgive like you. Please go before us and make the crooked places straight. (Isa 45v2) The eyes of the Lord are upon the righteous, and his ears attend to their prayers, but the face of the Lord is against those who do evil. (Psalms 34v10-12) Father, you said that if we ask for forgiveness that you would be faithful and just to forgive us and to cleanse us from all unrighteousness. (1 John 1v9) Father, today we come lifting our enemies to you. Father, we come asking that you would turn the hearts and minds of our enemies to you. We pray for divine intervention for every matter. We pray Father that you would save them, heal them, and deliver them Oh God from the grips of the enemy. Father, you said to love our enemies. Father, teach us to love as you love. Father, you loved us so much that you gave your only begotten son. (John 3v16) Father, you said to bless and curse not. Father, you commanded us do good to them that hate us, and to pray for those who despitefully use us and persecute us. (Matt 5) Father, you said if thine enemy be hungry give him bread, and if he be thirsty give him drink: For in doing so thou shalt heap coals of fire upon his head, and the Lord shall reward thee. (Prov. 25v21-22) Father, you also said you will prepare a table before me in the presence of my enemies, you will anoint our head with oil and our cup will run over. (Psalms 23) Father help us to be strong in the Lord and the power of your might. Father, help us to put on the full armor of God so that we may be able to stand in the evil day. Father, help us to realize that our fight isn't against flesh and blood. Help us to remember that we are fighting against principalities, powers, rulers of darkness and spiritual wickedness in high place. (Ephe. 6v10-13) Help us to target the enemy behind the scene that's controlling these people. Help us Oh God! Father, we pray that you will go before us to remove every snare, every trap, every scheme, every evil plan of the enemy. Father, give us your wisdom, your insight and a strong discerning eye. Father, you said we have not because we asked not. Father, thank you for your eyes being on us and your ears are open to our prayer. We ask you all these things in your son Jesus' name. Amen.

Notes to Self

I Sing the Mighty Power of God
I sing the mighty pow'r of God,
That made the mountains rise,
That spread the flowing seas abroad,
And built the lofty skies.

I sing the wisdom that ordained the sun
To rule the day;
The moon shines full at His command,
And all the stars obey.

No Weapon Formed Against Me – see lyrics on line
(Written by Andre Ray)

I Told the Storm – see lyrics on line
(Various Performers)

PRAYER FOR PROTECTION

Let us sing our 3 Worship songs to Usher us into the Presence of God:

I Sing the Mighty Power of God
No Weapon Formed Against Us
I Told the Storm

Prayer: Heavenly Father we come before your throne of grace today to say thank you. Thank you for life, health and strength. Thank you for your grace and mercy. Thank you for never leaving us and never forsaking us. Thank you for the roof over our head. Thank you for the clothes on our back and the shoes for our feet. Thank you for clean running water. Thank you that all our bills are paid, and all of our needs are met. Thank you for watching over us on last night as we slept and slumbered. Father, we realize that someone didn't wake up to day. Father, we realize that someone woke up this morning in a hospital bed. Father, we realize someone woke up this morning and couldn't feed their children. Father, we pray and ask you to meet the needs of these people who are dealing with adverse situations today. Father, we pray that you would comfort the bereaving family, heal the body of that one in the hospital, and provide finances to that one that need food for their children. We ask you Father, to forgive us of our sins. Father, forgive us for our sins of omission as well as our sins of commissions. Father, we pray that you would wash us, purge us, and cleanse of all unrighteousness create in us clean hands and a pure heart. (Psalms 51) Father, you said that if we ask for forgiveness that you would be faithful and just to forgive us and to cleanse us from all unrighteousness. (1 John 1v9) Father we come today praying for protection for us and our families. Father, we pray that you would build a hedge of protection around us and our families. (Job 1v10) Father, we pray that you would fill our mouth with songs of deliverance. Father we pray that you would shield us with your feathers and hide us under your wings. (Psalms 91v4) Father, we pray that you would go before us to make crooked places straight. (Isa 45v2) We thank you for your angels that are encamped about us because we fear you. Your word said that when the enemy comes in like a flood the spirit of the Lord would raise up a standard against him. We thank you because your word said that when the enemy come against us one way he would have to flee seven different ways. Father, your word says that greater is he who is in us than he who is in the world. Father, we pray that you will continue to hold us in the hollow of your hand. (Isa 49v2) Father, we thank you for being our tower of strength. Father, we thank you for you are our glory and the lifter of our heads. Father, we pray that you would be our strong tower, our refuge and our shield and buckler. Father, protect us from the dangers we know of and those we don't know of. Father, you said you would contend with those that contend with us. (Isa 49v25) Father, we thank you because you said that you would watch over your word to perform it. (Jere 1v12) You said no weapon formed against us shall prosper and every tongue risen against us in judgement we shall condemn. (Isa 54v17) Father your word says that your promises are yes and amen. You are not a man that you should lie neither are you the son of man that you should repent, if you said it you will bring it to pass, if you spoke it you will make it good. (Numb 23v19) Father, we thank you for your protection. You said we have not because we ask not but we are asking today in the name of your son Jesus. Amen

Notes to Self

I Must Tell Jesus
I must tell Jesus all of my trials;
I cannot bear these burdens alone;
In my distress He kindly will help me;
He ever loves and cares for His own. I must tell Jesus! I must tell Jesus!
I cannot bear my burdens alone;
I must tell Jesus! I must tell Jesus!
Jesus can help me, Jesus alone.

I must tell Jesus all of my troubles;

Father Can You Hear Me – see lyrics on line
(Various Performers)

I Love you Lord, and I lift my Voice – see lyrics on line
(Various Performers)

PRAYERS FOR OVERCOMING DISTRACTIONS

Let us sing our 3 Worship songs to Usher us into the Presence of God:

I Must Tell Jesus
Father Can You Hear Me
I Love You Lord and I Lift My Voice

Prayer: Heavenly Father we come before your throne of grace today as humble as we know how. We come in a spirit of thanksgiving, praise, and honor. All the praises, glory and honor are due to your name. Father, we come bowing my heart in your presence as we say thank you. Father, we thank you for life, health, and strength. Father, we thank you for the use of our limbs. Father, we thank you for the blood running warm in our veins. We thank you for the healing of our body. We thank you for every organ operating the way you created it to operate. Thank you, Father! This is the day that the Lord hath made and we will rejoice and be glad in it. (Psalms 118v24) This is a day that we have never seen before. Father, we thank you for saving us and our extended family. We thank you for leading us, guiding us and protecting us. We thank you for your continuous blessings. Father, you bless us even when we don't deserve it. Father, we need you! We can't make it on our own. We need your help God! We realize that we can do nothing without you God. Father, have mercy on us! We need your wisdom, your guidance, your love and your strength. Father, please forgive us for our sins. Father wash us, purge us, cleanse us from all unrighteousness and create in us a clean heart and renew a right spirit within us Jesus. Father, you said if we ask for forgiveness you would be faithful and just to forgive us and cleanse of all unrighteousness. (1 John 1v9) Father, today we come to you asking for your help to deliver us from these distractions. Father, we are struggling as we are trying to keep our hearts and minds fixed on you and this journey. Father, we are asking you Oh God to set our faces like flint. And we know we should not be ashamed. (Isa 50v7) Please keep us from looking to the left or the right. Father, help us to keep our eyes on Jesus because he is the author and the finisher of our faith. Who for the joy set before him endured the cross, despising the shame is set down at the right hand of God. (Heb. 12v2) The scriptures say, "Look unto me, and be ye saved, all the ends of the earth; for I am God, and there is none else. I have sworn by myself, the word has gone out of my mouth in righteousness and shall not return. That unto me every knee shall bow, and every tongue confess that Jesus is Lord. (Isa. 45v22) Father, we need your help! Help us to press toward the prize of the mark of the high calling of God which is in Christ Jesus. (Phillip 3v14) Father, you said that this race isn't given to the swift nor the strong but for those who will endure to the end. (Ecc. 9v11) We pray for a spirit of endurance Oh God! Father, we will not faint in the day of adversity because our strength is large. Father, we are leaning and depending on you to be with us. Father, you are our shepherd and we shall not want. You maketh us to lie down in green pastures. You leadeth us beside the still water. You restored our soul. He leadeth me in paths of righteousness for his name sake. Yea though I walk through the shadows of death I will fear no evil for thou art with me. Thy rod and thy staff they comfort me. Thou preparest a table before me in the presence of mine enemies. Thou anointest my head with oil my cup runneth over. Surely goodness and mercy shall follow me all the days of my life and I shalt dwell in thine house forever. (Psalms 23)

Notes to Self

Printed in the United States
By Bookmasters